May ██████ ██████ go
Strength to Streng.--.

Best wishes from,

Avril, Allan and
Colin ████████

WOMEN'S LACROSSE

The Skills of the Game

WOMEN'S LACROSSE

The Skills of the Game

BOBBIE TRAFFORD
and
KATH HOWARTH

THE CROWOOD PRESS

First published in 1989 by
The Crowood Press
Ramsbury, Marlborough,
Wiltshire SN8 2HE

British Library Cataloguing in Publication Data

Howarth, Kath
   Women's lacrosse: the skills of the game.
   1. Women's lacrosse — Manuals
   I. Title   II. Trafford, Bobbie
   796.34'7

ISBN 1 85223 194 7

Acknowledgements

The authors wish to thank Phil Collier and Carole Kleinfelder for their
invaluable contributions to the way they think about lacrosse.
Thanks also to the 1988 England squad for their generous help in
the photographic sessions, to Paula Pimbley, Jean Arnold and Paul
Whelan for their help with the final checking of the text and to Lynda
Marsden for typing the manuscript.

Cover photographs, frontispiece and Figs 32, 123 and 124 by
Eileen Langsley.
Fig 22 by Roger Owens.
Figs 125 and 126 courtesy of the AEWLA (Fig 125 by
M. Wohlwender).
Demonstration photographs by Ken Travis of Liverpool Polytechnic.
Line-drawings by Janet Sparrow.

Typeset by Keyboard Services, Luton
Printed in Great Britain by The Bath Press

Contents

Bobbie Trafford and Kath Howarth are the two foremost coaches in women's lacrosse in England.

In this book they have analysed the game as it is played today and suggested ways for developing players for the 1990s and beyond who are adaptable and flexible both technically and tactically.

Players, coaches and teachers will find coaching philosophy expressed here which emphasises building a team that not only has the technical skills, but also understands the game as a whole and knows how to work together positively.

Yvonne Neild
President, All England Women's Lacrosse Association

With obvious sense and absorbing enthusiasm, Bobbie Trafford and Kath Howarth present their approach to the many possibilities within women's lacrosse in a way that shows the direction the game will take in the future.

Their book is invaluable for both established players and those interested in improving their understanding of this rapidly developing game – a must for anyone wishing to enjoy the full fascinations of lacrosse.

Jan Guilbride
Former England and Great Britain captain

Bobbie Trafford, the England Women's Lacrosse Coach, has been involved in playing, coaching and umpiring the game at every level for many years. As well as being National Coach, she is an international umpire and has officiated at both the 1982 and 1986 World Cups. She represented England at the International Federation of Women's Lacrosse Associations (IFWLA) from 1982 until 1987, and toured as umpire with the GB tour to Australia and as coach with the 1988 tour to the USA.

Kath Howarth, currently senior lecturer in Physical Education at Liverpool, is the Assistant England Coach. She represented England and Great Britain as a player and was Assistant England Coach at the 1986 World Cup. Since December of that year she has coached England with Bobbie Trafford, both on the USA tour, and at the World Cup, Australia in 1989. From 1982 until 1986 she was Secretary/Treasurer of the IFWLA and is now Vice-President of the All England Women's Lacrosse Association (AEWLA).

Introduction

Lacrosse has come a long way since the first forms of the game were seen being played by native Indians in North America. It is not now played over miles of ground, does not have hundreds of players, nor is it used anymore as a means of training Indian warriors. However, lacrosse has still retained the characteristics of the free-flowing, running game that originally made it an ideal setting for developing endurance for war and hunting expeditions.

Today's game has developed into several forms, notably men's lacrosse, which is a contact sport requiring protective equipment for all players, and the women's non-contact version, where only the goalkeeper is allowed to wear protective clothing. In addition, there is 'pop-lacrosse' and other similar adapted games which are ideal as introductions for beginners. Such games do not allow contact at all, and can be used with mixed groups before they move on to the separate men's and women's games. Adult mixed lacrosse rules are also in operation, as is a wheelchair version of the game. Thus lacrosse caters for every possible group which may be attracted by this unusual and exciting game.

The women's game is developing fast, both through the adapted games played at grass-roots, school and club level, and through the adult game played at international level. Since the first World Cup was run, under the auspices of the International Federation of Women's Lacrosse Associations (IFWLA), in Nottingham in 1982, there has been a tremendous upsurge of interest in developing and standardising international rules, organising an increased number of international tours and events, and promoting the development of the game in new countries.

Rules are reviewed after each World Cup, and therefore every four years there is the opportunity to suggest rule changes in the light of the fast development of the game. This book is based upon the rules and interpretations of the 1986 Rules Book, and readers should check with the appropriate Association whether changes have occurred since then.

The area of play *(Fig 1)* is set out to encourage the open nature of the game,

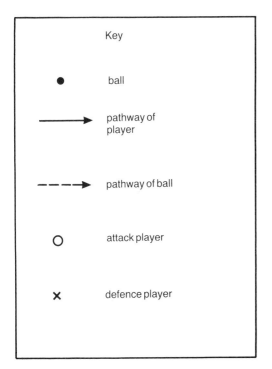

Key

●   ball

——▶   pathway of player

– – –▶   pathway of ball

○   attack player

✕   defence player

Introduction

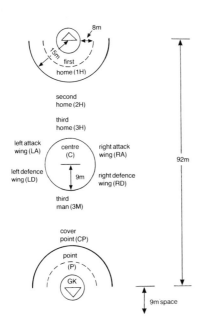

Fig 1   Field layout and positions.

having no set boundaries other than a minimum size of area and natural boundaries agreed by umpires and players. The umpire's whistle stops the game at its edges and the player nearest the ball is given possession. It is quite possible that this spatial freedom will become more limited as rules develop and increased fitness allows players to move over greater areas into defence and attack.

The shape of the game is rather like a diamond, with play moving out from the goalkeeper to the wings and then focusing in towards the goal. The players are, at present, unrestricted in where they can move, and one of the unusual characteristics of the game is that play continues around the back of the goal. Rules have evolved in order to keep the space in front of goal uncluttered and open, and it is this area

of the game that is likely to be the focus of rule development. Most games have developed spatial, time or numerical limitations to overcome the problem of blocking up the goal area. Rules need to work to maintain the character of the sport with the least amount of interference. Not an easy task.

As a non-contact game, the other area of focus for the rules is that governing what defences and attacks can and cannot do in positioning and moving with or without the ball. Rule interpretations on tackling the stick, marking players and blocking pathways are crucial, and should be clearly understood by players and coaches as well as umpires. In a fast running game, such as lacrosse, some moves can be dangerous when defences or attacks are on the blind side of a player. Rules therefore have to carefully differentiate between the safe and dangerous tackle, 'pick', or shot. Such interpretations are the most difficult for umpires since they are calls requiring judgement.

This book represents our beliefs about the way in which today's game for women is developing and how it can best be coached. It is aimed at coaching players rather than introducing the game to beginners, and will, we hope, be useful for both players and coaches to read. It builds on the tactical and technical experience that beginners obtain from playing small-sided games as proosed in the AEWLA/ELU preliminary coaching award scheme. It is concerned that techniques are learnt in order to play the game effectively rather than as ends in themselves.

Our approach may be rather different from that found in other coaching manuals. There are no lists of how to perform basic techniques since we are anxious to avoid presenting a stereotyped view of 'correct stickwork'. Our questions have focused more on judging whether and how stickwork can be effective and efficient within the game. Does it work? Is it safe? Is it appropriate to the situation? Skills develop only because they are required in the game which is a constantly changing environment for every player. We want to avoid the situation where a player, for example, automatically pulls her stick from one side of her body to the other, without reference to the defence's position, just because that is how she has always practised dodging. We also want to challenge the idea that, for example, only certain ways of holding the stick are acceptable. Certainly there are times when not slipping the hand down the stick is advisable for control and accuracy, but sometimes an extended stick, with a slipped top hand or only one hand on, is vital in the game. The question should be whether it was used at the right time, and whether it extends the player's potential on the field.

Such questions require an approach to practising that involves the players in making the sort of decisions required of them in the game. Thus, in both the skills chapters and the team-play chapters, the emphasis has been placed upon 'why?', 'when?' and 'where?' rather than 'how?'. This is not an encouragement to forget the technical aspects of the game. Indeed, those very questions cause many technical problems to arise which then have to be solved and mastered and added to the player's increasingly complex repertoire of game knowledge.

It is important that the ideas expressed in this book are seen as a stepping-stone for further thought and debate about the future direction of lacrosse. A flexible, non-stereotyped attitude is essential if players, coaches and spectators alike are really to appreciate the complexity and breadth of the game today.

Appreciating why things happen in a game, understanding the restrictions that a unit of defences is placing on the opposition or the clever combinations which result in a goal, will help everyone concerned with lacrosse to greater enjoyment.

We hope this book will play a part in developing that understanding and thereby help readers to appreciate more fully the greatest game of all:

Lacrosse, fastest game on two feet.

1 Attacking Skills

KEEPING POSSESSION

Safe team possession is the key to scoring goals. A player with the ball has 100 per cent possession and must realise the value of her situation. The ball carrier is the decision maker and it is her team-mates' responsibility to give her good passing options. Some players give away the greatest advantage of safe possession by sending the ball into a 50/50 situation. Patience is a virtue for the team in possession of the ball. If the passing lane, between the passer and receiver's stick, is not open, don't pass. If the goal cut is covered, don't feed. If the angle or shooting space is not there, don't shoot. The ability to make correct decisions is fundamental to keeping safe possession. The exciting game which we all love to watch comes when all the decisions are sound and the ball travels fluently into the goal.

Keeping possession involves a combination of the following skills:

1. Safe protection of the ball, including:
   (a) stick flexibility,
   (b) good footwork and dodging,
   (c) body flexibility.
2. Safe passing, requiring:
   (a) communication,
   (b) choosing the best pass,
   (c) a clear passing lane,
   (d) precision and accuracy.
3. Safe receiving, requiring:
   (a) space making,
   (b) signalling,
   (c) extension and 'give' behind the flight of the ball.

Safe Protection of the Ball

Stick Flexibility

A defence can only occupy a portion of the ball carrier's personal space. Keeping the stick head well away from the defence is a vital basic skill. The stick is a natural extension of the body, not an appendage, and a player should be able to move the ball anywhere around her body to avoid the defence's stick. This requires great stick and wrist flexibility; changing the top hand, extending the stick away from the body one handed and bringing the stick close, low or high, are all going to be necessary at some point in the game. An attacker who is aware of her defence constantly manoeuvres her stick into a safe position whilst deciding what to do next. Ask these questions:

● Where is your defence?
● Where is your free space?
● Is your head up and are you looking for possibilities?

Good Footwork and Dodging

Keeping the ball away from the defence usually requires movement of the feet as well as the stick. Change of pace, sudden acceleration, change of direction, as well as stick movement, can all give the ball carrier more space and time to make decisions. A player with the ball is responsible for not making bodily contact with a defence and must be in control and balanced when moving with the ball. Sometimes the best option is to keep possession and run, because the space ahead is open or there is only one defender ahead to consider. Go for goal! This can be very threatening even when it happens far away from the critical scoring area round the goal. A defence driving through the midfield with the ball or an attack taking on the defence at 15m both show their team's determination to turn team possession into a successful goal. Some players show determination in the wrong way, barging into defences in their effort to progress the ball upfield or to take a shot. This is where good footwork pays off to wrong-foot the defence. It is vital that the ball carrier gives no indication as to the direction of the dodge until as late as possible. A sideways 'stutter-step' just before reaching an opponent, a strong fake to one side followed by fast acceleration, or a slight falter in speed to draw a defence before driving past, are all signs of good attack play. The combination of flexible stickwork and sound footwork makes for safe individual possession. The attack must run straight at the defence and deliberately set about making her unsure and off balance, because she needs to change and adjust her position at the last minute.

Sometimes the chosen pathway is blocked and passing options are not clear. The ball carrier needs to slow or even stop her feet to maintain possession and avoid the tackle. Very often as the stick is pulled back away from the defence a roll dodge can be made (*Fig 2*), thus opening up new passing lanes, or even allowing the ball carrier to find a new pathway to the target whilst at the same time protecting the stick. Changing the top hand is useful protection and opens up the free space for a pass.

Sometimes a player has quickly to adjust her position merely to keep possession and

Fig 2(a)   Roll dodge. The attack's dodge to the right is blocked.

Fig 2(b)   The attack rolls back to protect the stick, changing hands.

Fig 2(c)   The attack drives to the left with the stick held away from the tackle.

look for help, for example if pressed by two defences. Here again, good footwork is vital to get the player away and free the stick for a quick pass.

Body Flexibility

Good shoulder and trunk flexibility are useful both for protecting the stick by twisting, stretching, dipping and weaving and also for deceiving an opponent. The ability to move the body laterally is especially useful when faking and feinting before dodging, passing or shooting.

SAFE PASSING   (Figs 3–9)

The ball travels fastest to goal through the air and in a straight line. If only it were as simple as that! Passing the ball gives the

Fig 2(d)   The attack finds the space.

opponents a chance of possession. So let us think first what makes a pass really safe.

1. There must be communication. This usually means eye contact with the receiver, though experienced players may try to deceive the opposition by disguising this signal.

2. The target stick head must be open and available.

3. There must be a passing lane (*Fig 3*) into which no defence's stick can reach.

4. The pass must be precise. The receiver signals a target which the passer homes into with speed and accuracy. The passer must be able to send the ball wherever the receiver asks for it. The ability to pass to and from any level is crucial. Timing is vital – a delay can result in an interception or a tackle

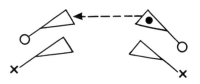

Fig 3(a)   Passing lane open.

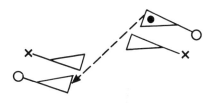

Fig 3(b)   Passing lane covered.

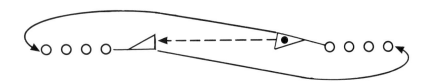

Fig 4(a)   Shuttle. Run towards the ball for a flat, hard pass. Join opposite line.

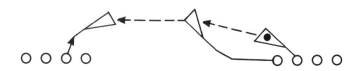

Fig 4(b)   'Going away' shuttle. No. 1 passes flat, angled pass to No. 2. No. 2 passes to No. 3 who sends flat 'going-away' pass to No. 4.

Fig 5 Connecting cut.

– too early a pass can put the receiver under undue pressure. The weight of the pass needs to be right for the situation. The firm flat pass is more difficult to intercept and therefore very safe, but the looping, high pass may be necessary to swing the ball across the field or to send the ball behind the goal.

5.   The pass must be the best choice given all the circumstances. Loud calls from a team-mate may distract and cause a wrong decision. It may just be a fake to deflect an opponent's attention. The final decisions must be made calmly by the ball carrier, who can see all the options available.

Passing safely and accurately should be practised continually. Shuttles can be useful repetitive practices. (*Fig 4*)

Fig 6 A connecting cut.

Various situations on the field need constant practice for passing accuracy.

(a)   The pass to the connecting cut (*Figs 5 & 6*) is used to connect the midfield. The attack cuts to the ball and a flat direct pass to a low stick is required. The defence is behind the receiver, therefore it is vital that the pass is not high, thus putting the receiver's stick in a vulnerable position for the tackle.

(b)   The pass to the goal cut (*Fig 7*) where the attack cuts away from the ball at an angle. The pass is still flat and direct but needs more weight and distance. This is a fine-angled and difficult pass but puts the receiver in an excellent attacking position. (See the section on shooting in this chapter.)

(c)   The feed from behind goal. The attack cuts towards the ball and the goal. The feeder (*Fig 8*) must first decide whether the cutter is open and then feed with perfect accuracy and timing exactly to the stick.

There is no room here for mistakes. The feeder must be extremely patient and must not be rushed into poor passing in which possession can be lost.

(c)   Passing to the free side/non defended space (*Fig 9*), e.g. a player on the wing rolls back and turns in towards the middle of the game, or a player stopped by a double team passes back into the 'trailing' space behind her.

SAFE RECEIVING

Safe receiving is the result of a great deal of hard work: positioning and repositioning, cutting and recutting in order that the stick is made available in an open passing lane. Catching must be safe and sure. The target head of the stick must be open behind the line of the flight of the ball. The passing game requires the ball to be sent hard, direct and flat. The receiver needs first to absorb the power of the pass before she can cradle, pass or shoot. She must feel the weight of the ball and absorb the power. The greater the force of the pass, the more give is required before redirecting the force.

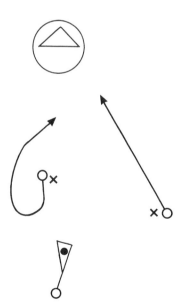

Fig 7   Goal cuts.

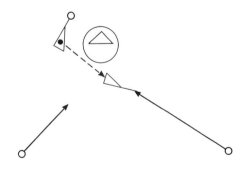

Fig 8   Feed to a cutter.

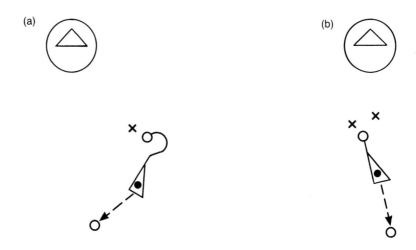

Fig 9   Passing to the non-defended side.

Snatching or wrapping movements of the stick head are inappropriate for the firm flat pass. In a very few situations where the ball is looped softly or rising it may be necessary to move to the ball to take it away from danger and protect the stick head from an opponent. Examples would be a throw where two players are trying to collect the ball and move away from the tackle, the draw which sometimes goes upwards between the two centres, or a flick-up pass to an adjacent player running through. In these cases there is little force to absorb and the stick moves to the ball to gain possession as early as possible.

A player needs to be able to receive the ball anywhere around her body. This involves the ability to change hands, which opens up the space on either side of the body for receiving and, therefore, sending the ball. Receiving and sending skills should be practised from the earliest time with either hand at the top of the stick. This is the beginning of total flexibility where a player is able to take the pass anywhere around the body and convert it to her team's advantage. It is unrealistic to practise receiving the ball only at one level since this will never happen in the game. The ability to present the target near and far from the body, medium and low, depending on circumstances, and to take the ball confidently and safely is the mark of a player who can turn any chance into a shot, a good pass or safe possession. This needs to be practised in situations of increasing pressure. A player should be encouraged to see the need to avoid difficulties by accelerating as she receives, protecting the stick head and generally being aware of space and opponents.

There are two important aspects of safe receiving which occur prior to the catch. These are: 1. Space making, and 2. Signalling.

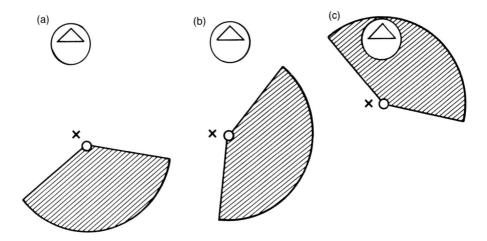

Fig 10   Every attack has a free side.

Space Making   *(Figs 10 & 11)*

Any potential receiver should ask themselves first, 'What space is my defence giving me?' They should seek to minimise the effect a defence can have on the moment of reception. First of all, the position of the defence must be assessed in relation to the ball carrier.

The next question is, 'How can I make more of that space?' Every attack has a free side *(Fig 10)* and she must work to increase the potential of that free side by making the available space larger. This always involves a preparatory movement away from that space, followed by a cut or a clear signal to receive in it. This first movement relates entirely to the defence's chosen marking position. If she marks behind you, take her even further back to increase your space ahead. If she marks your right side, take her forward right to increase space diagonally left. Changing hands will further increase the space available. If she marks in front, take her forwards to increase the space behind. *(Fig 11)*.

The preparatory movement usually leads directly into the cut so that the defence is wrong-footed. Sometimes, however, an attack may move the defence away from the chosen space, and hold that space until the optimum moment for the cut. In a restricted space the movement involved may be very small and the held position resolved merely by a lunge and an appropriate signal into the available space.

Signalling

Sending and receiving safely require communication between players. This may take the form of:

1.   Clear eye contact between sender and receiver.

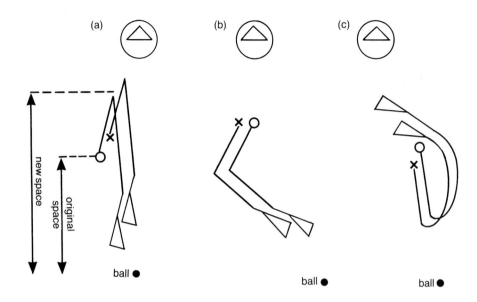

Fig 11(a) Creating space. Player marking behind.
Fig 11(b) Player marking to the side.
Fig 11(c) Player marking in front.

2.   A firmly presented stick head as a target for the sender.

3.   Calling to establish availability.

4.   Preparation of the sender's body and stick in readiness for sending.

These are all 'cues' or signals that a player needs to learn to recognise and be able to select from the mass of information that crowds in from the environment. When beginners first start to learn a new game there are many demands on their attention, but gradually they learn to be selective in what they see or perceive. The coach, in this instance, can help this process by identifying to both the ball carrier and the receiver the specific signals or cues which will help them make correct decisions. The excellent games player can process this information quickly, but reminders about cues and signals for decision making should constantly be given even to experienced players.

1.   Eye Contact

'Head up – eyes open!' From the very beginning, players with the ball should be encouraged to look up and look around. Only then can other players signal to them. They must search and scan the field for the best cut and the clearest signal as they move and protect the ball from their defender. 'Heads on swivels!'

Having adjusted and made space, the receiver actively seeks eye contact to signal her readiness to receive the ball. This should be done as soon as possible to allow the sender the earliest chance to pass the ball.

Sometimes when making space, the receiver cuts forward and then rolls away at an angle for the 'going-away' pass. In this case it is essential that the receiver's head turns very quickly to look at the sender giving the cue for the pass.

Another example would be in defence when players cut out and away for the goal clear. Eye contact must be made between the goalkeeper and the receiver.

Sometimes experienced players will exploit knowledge of this signal to deceive the opposition. For example, they may look in one direction and send the ball in another. This could be used in shooting or to confuse the defender covering the passing line. This requires great understanding and sensitivity between players who are used to playing together.

Fig 12(a) Opening the stick face to make a clear target for the pass.

2. The Target *(Fig 12)*

The stick head of the receiver needs to be open to the ball and held as still as possible so that the sender sees a clear, large target. When manoeuvring for position and making space, the receiver's stick will be held in a relaxed manner. By suddenly extending the arm and fixing the top wrist the stick head becomes obviously presented as a target and attracts the attention of the sender.

This extension is the prerequisite of a safe catch, since it allows the receiver then to give behind the line of flight. Of course, it is possible to receive close to the body but this is a more difficult skill. It is the responsibility of the receiver to present the target exactly where they wish to receive the ball. The receiver must signal so that the defender is unable to intercept the pass, or tackle on the catch. The target can be presented at any level, on either side of the body, with either hand leading. It can be held near or far from the body. This variety is particularly import-

Fig 12(b) A more difficult presentation of the stick for the sender.

ant in the critical scoring area. (See the following section on shooting.)

The timing of this signal is crucial. It must be synchronised with the ability of the sender to release the ball. If the initial target presentation is not immediately used the receiver must work and reposition to make herself available for a later pass. Once the moment has gone, the target should be withdrawn to indicate to the sender that the receiver is now repositioning.

3. Calling

A verbal cue is sometimes necessary to attract the sender's attention. There is nothing wrong with calling if it is used appropriately, for example when a player is behind the ball carrier and available to help. This can be particularly useful when the ball carrier is under great pressure and does not have the time to scan and select.

Calling can also be used in a planned tactic positively to deceive the opposition.

4. Sender's Preparation

The receiver should look for the sender's readiness to release the ball. Is the sender's head up and the ball safely in the stick? Is she balanced and in control bodily? An experienced player will also recognise moments when this state of readiness cannot be achieved and will move in anticipation of the need to flick or push the ball to the nearest player.

SHOOTING

Games are won by scoring more goals than the opponents and teams should take every opportunity to take valid shots. If you don't shoot you won't score! Shooting is an art which needs constantly practising, as beautiful team moves are often ruined by a poorly executed or ill-timed shot. Accuracy is far more important than power, and statistics show unfortunately that a high percentage of shots miss the goal completely. Every shot should at least be 'on the cage' and make the goalkeeper work for the save, rather than doing her job for her by missing altogether.

Often shooters have an urge to take fancy but wild shots. These shots may look spectacular and have the crowd on their feet, but the truth is that their success ratio is very poor, and they should not be encouraged.

Shooting cannot be considered in isolation but within a framework of:

● Cutting for the ball.
● Feeding the pass.
● The shots (a) Close-range.
          (b) Long, outside.

Cutting *(Figs 13–15)*

Good cutting for shooting is critical as this gives the attack their best scoring opportunities. The cutter is aiming to receive the feed right in front of goal.

Players should pull away from goal at the front to give themselves space for cutting in towards the goal-cage. When the ball is behind the goal the goalkeeper is at a great disadvantage as she must turn to see the ball. She needs to turn to watch the feeder behind goal and the quick feeding foward pass gives her little reaction time for the cutter's shot. Players should be aware of the optimum cutting lanes, or channels of space, which cross in the critical scoring area or 'hole'. *(Fig 13)*. It is important to cut only when the feeder is in a good position to feed you, i.e. when the ball is opposite you at the other end of a cutting channel and you

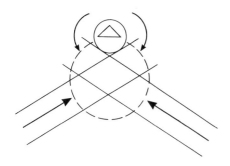

Fig 13   Cutting channels into the 'hole'.

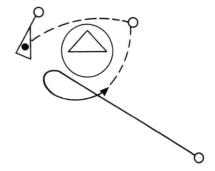

Fig 14   Cutter rolls back after initial cut to receive the feed.

can move towards it. Some players cut to areas where it is impossible to receive a pass.

The best time to cut is when your defender's eyes leave you to check the ball.

Players should work hard to gain a step or two on their defence by possibly faking to one side of the defence and breaking forward to the opposite side, or by stutter-stepping at the defender's body and, when they lean, driving and accelerating the other way. In fact, any time a defender slides in to back up other defences and their attention leaves you, cut behind them through the back door space. A cutter's stick should be held into the body initially and then held out as a target as they gain a step. While actually cutting, the stick should be held still and positioned where you want to receive. It is unrealistic in the game today to have a greatly extended stick in the 'hole' area (the space in front of the goal) as there are too many defenders waiting to tackle. Players

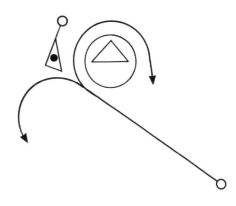

Fig 15   Cutting and repositioning if the feed is not made.

15

need to learn to ask for, and expect, the ball very close to the body.

If a cutter does not receive the ball initially, they can roll back, changing hands, and ask the feeder on the opposite side of the goal, or get out and reposition to balance the attacking group, clearing the area for other players to make cuts. (*Figs 14 & 15*).

Feeding   *(Figs 16 & 17)*

Passing a ball to a player breaking or cutting towards goal is referred to as 'feeding'.

The majority of feeds occur when an initial attacking move has broken down and play has settled round the goal. A feed may come from behind the goal circle, usually from the sides of the goal-cage, or from anywhere in front of the goal. (*Figs 16 & 17*). The feeder needs to be relatively close to the cutter in order to get the ball to her

quickly, and the pass needs to be flat and fast. If the distance is too great, or the pass slow, a defence will easily intercept or get into a position to block the shot.

Feeders behind goal should keep to the sides, otherwise it is too easy for a goalkeeper to intercept a pass given from directly behind the goal, and the feeder's view can be restricted.

The feeder must always keep her defence guessing. The defence must feel that the feeder could dodge and drive for goal at any moment. To keep the defence guessing, keep moving, switch hands, drive to left or right and turn back on yourself, run at the defence then step back to make space. A drive on your defence at the beginning of the game makes her wary of you throughout the match.

Feeders can make the most of the space behind goal, since defenders do not always close mark and wait on the crease ready to take on the attack if she drives round. Even when defences do put pressure on the attack, they have a difficult task because of the danger of being wrong-footed around the circle edge. However, a defence is never challenged by an attack who remains static with the ball, and movement, even in a restricted space, is important.

One of the key attributes of a good feeder is patience. She is the decision-maker and must constantly watch the area directly in front of goal, rather than becoming engrossed in where she is in relation to her own defender. There is usually only a split second available when the cutter can receive the ball, and the feeder needs to be alert and anticipate the stick being open. Teammates should be working hard to make themselves available for the ball in a shooting position, but it is the feeder who selects the right moment.

Keeping the stick free and open, ready to

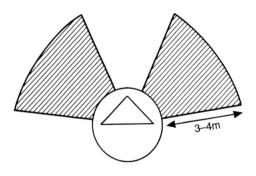

Fig 16   *Positioning of feeders behind the goal.*

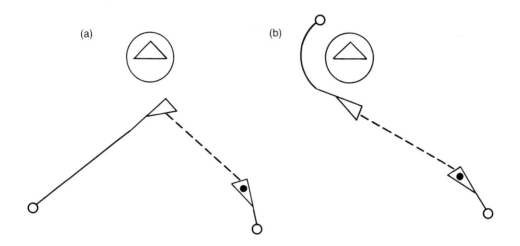

Fig 17   *Feeding from in front of the goal.*

give the feed, is crucial. There are many ways of doing this. Keep the stick well back behind the body and away from the defence to avoid stick handle checks. Do a quick fake movement with either the head or the stick immediately before releasing the ball. Make a quick change of level to free the stick head and remove pressure from the actual pass. Be able to feed with either the left or right hand at the top of the stick. This, added to the change of level, means that you have great flexibility and can feed from the side of the body furthest from the goal circle, thus gaining space and a good angle for the feed.

Looking for the target means looking not just at the cutter, but specifically aiming for the stick head which could be presented anywhere around the cutter's body. Accuracy is the key consideration when time and space are at a premium. This also means

accuracy of whatever pass is chosen, whether it is an overarm, side sling, flick or scoop. Obviously the overarm is usually the flatter, faster pass, but a defence does not always allow the best option.

The Shots

Shooting involves the mastery of a range of different shots. If an attack has one favourite shot, a good defence will soon assess this and make that shot impossible to take. A good shooter takes the space she is given and can technically produce the appropriate shot. There is not much time to shoot in today's game, yet there is, paradoxically, more time than attacks sometimes give themselves. Shots must be made to count. A rushed, flashy or inaccurate shot is just one more way to lose possession. Sometimes a goalkeeper appears much better than she is

Attacking Skills

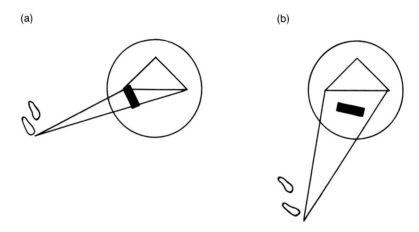

(a)   (b)

Fig 18   Shooting angles.   Fig 18(a)   No angle for a shot.
Fig 18(b)   Angle opening up for a shot.

because the attack are shooting the ball at her. Make the goalkeeper earn her keep. Every goalkeeper has a weaker side. Some goalies react very quickly to a stick movement, others take a 'set' position and wait for the ball to be released. Attacks should assess what the goalie's characteristics are, and what weaknesses she has shown. They must then play on those weaknesses.

A shooter should only shoot when she is ready. This means protecting the stick if you have the ball already, or feeling the weight of the ball as it enters your stick and counting 'one-two' before letting go. Accuracy in most cases is more important than velocity. Position in relation to the goal is vital; for example, when coming round the side of the goal, one more step might give you a better angle to shoot from. (*Fig 18*). The goalie will, at a certain point, have to commit herself and start to move, whereas one step before-

hand she can stay on her post and cover all the angles available.

There are times when a shot should be taken because key opponents are distracted for some reason. The goalkeeper may turn her head because she thinks you are too far out to take a shot. The defences may be sliding to cover each other and that moment of transition is their weakest time. The ball may be travelling from behind to in front of the goal. That is the moment when everyone, including the goalie, is having to reposition. All these moments give the perfect opportunity to shoot. Shots should be unexpected. A goalkeeper and the defence players follow the shooter's movements and particularly the stick head. Changing both the body position and the stick head can be confusing, as can changing the timing of the shot. So, suddenly change the level of the stick. If you receive high, drop the stick and shoot low. Change hands, particularly if you also change the direction of your feet. Shoot round the side of a defence if they hold their stick high. This may also unsight the goalkeeper. Fake a shot, then shoot as the goalie reacts. This is particularly useful when a player only has the goalkeeper to beat.

There are several different situations from which a team can score. These are:

1. Opportunist Goals

If the ball is loose in front of goal an alert attack can capitalise on this to score. Constant pressure by the attack can cause the defence to fumble the ball, or the ball may just be running loose, or have rebounded from the goalkeeper. There is no time for textbook stickwork if this half chance is to be converted into a shot. Players must be prepared to push, flick, catch or scoop it back into the net in the shortest possible time. Constant alertness for the slight chances that may arise is essential, and speed of reaction and agility are vital components to success. Stick skills relating to sending a ground ball into the goal need to be practised.

Practices

(a) One player gets six balls into the goal as quickly as possible. She should think about the angle available and the movement of the goalkeeper, for example, for a ball on the edge of the crease the player must avoid a crosse-over (*see* Glossary). Also, if the goalkeeper is contesting the ball as well, then the attack must control the ball and flick it over the goalkeeper's head into the net.

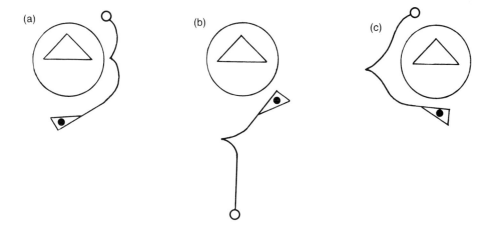

Fig 19   Dodging round the crease.

(b) A feeder rolls a ball through the circle, as if it is a rebound from the goalkeeper's pads. This can be developed by adding a defence, then another attack and defence. Here the decision is, 'Can I score?' or 'Is it better to flick the ball to the other attack?' The second attack and defence off the ball must position for a flick or scoop, if they are needed.

2. Dodging and Driving on Goal *(Figs 19 & 20)*

Dodges are used to put an attack into the strongest shooting position when in possession. The dodge should move the player towards the goal and open up their strongest shot. Left-hand-up players often drive and dodge from behind goal round the left post, thus allowing an early shot from the left side. A strong right-handed shooter will pull the defence left as they approach the goal and stutter-step past on the right. This is not to say that all attacks should not work hard to become equally strong from both sides of the body since there will be times when they are forced by excellent defences onto their weaker side.

Sometimes an attack tempts the defence to commit to a tackle. It is at that moment that space opens up for a dodge and shot. (*Fig 19*). This can be used when driving from behind goal to gain the inside line round the circle. A player needs to be aware of the available space around the crease. If the defence forces them wide and away from a shooting angle, the inside dodge can be used. This could be a roll dodge or a face-on dodge, with a quick change of hand to protect the stick. (*Fig 20*). If the attack manages to dodge close to the crease but the defence is still covering that space, she can roll outside and create a scoring angle, shooting with a low, whipping shot.

Fig 20(a)   *Attack driving round the crease. The attack drives round. The defence steers.*

Fig 20(b)   *The attack is forced off a shooting line and rolls back.*

Fig 20(c)   The attack changes hands to protect the stick.

3.   Receiving and Shooting
(Figs 21 & 22)

Receiving the ball after a good clean cut towards goal with an open stick, followed by an immediate shot, is the kind of play that people tend to think of as 'real shooting'. However, other methods as described earlier are just as valid and just as important in getting the ball into the back of the net.

Nowadays the long free run to receive the ball in an extended stick is a rarity near the goal. An extended stick is likely to be tackled and players need to practise receiving on both sides of the body near the ear. They should also practise shooting with right and left hands at the top. From the very start players should be encouraged to be equally confident to shoot from both sides of the body. This makes them a much greater threat and gives them many more shooting options around the goal.

When receiving a feed, which is usually sent hard and fast, the top hand needs to be near the throat of the stick, yet slightly relaxed to allow for the extra 'give' needed to cushion the ball. Although sometimes the stick has to be extended, for example upwards, to take a high ball in the only available space, the regular positioning of the top hand near the throat of the stick helps in the following ways:

1.   It makes it easier to catch and control bad feeds.
2.   It makes the ensuing shot more accurate.
3.   It is easier to protect the stick head.
4.   It is easier to play with the weaker hand.

A shot that immediately follows the 'give' on reception of the ball is called a 'quick-stick' shot. It is effective in that a shot can be taken before defence and goalkeeper have repositioned or focused on the stick head. The danger is, however, that some attacks think about the shot before the catch has been controlled properly and mistime the release. Make sure as you practise that you feel the weight of the ball and only then redirect the force.

In the game give yourself a word like 'careful' between the two phases of the shot. The shot is quick but it must not be hurried.

The quick-stick shot often occurs near to the goal. Care should be taken on any shot near the goal crease to reduce the follow through. The action is a *punch* with the top hand and a *pull* with the bottom hand, followed immediately by a pull back. Body and stick need to keep from crossing over the crease.

The best area to receive and shoot is in the centre of the 'hole' (*Fig 21*) where an attack has a good chance of scoring. The angles are good in that the shot can go high, medium or low on either side of the goalie.

Attacking Skills

The distance is not so great that the goalie has time to react.

Timing is crucial since the ball needs to be received and shot whilst still in the area with the greatest options for the shot. Placing the shot is also important. The goalkeeper's non-stick side is usually her weakest, particularly the middle level which is difficult to cover with the stick. Some players show a tremendous repertoire of shots because they practise and improve constantly. Variation of shot from within 8m is vital. These are just some examples of the variation available when receiving and shooting:

(a) Ask for the ball low, near the ankle, and lever the shot in from that level.

(b) Ask for the ball high, then drop the stick head as you run the ball forward.

(c) Ask for the ball at medium height, then sink by bending the knees and whip the stick through at knee level, or skim the ball to bounce low on the edge of the crease.

(d) Ask for the ball very high, if you are tall (*Fig 22*), and quick-stick from high into the top corner.

(e) Use the wrists to create a short, whipping action that can be deceptively placed high or low because there is little follow through.

(f) Fake a shot by moving the head or shoulder or stick head. Often just a shoulder movement leaves the stick poised for a quick shot once the goalie starts to react.

(g) Use the defender's body as a screen, then shoot round her thus concealing the stick from the goalkeeper until the moment of release.

(h) Do some of the above, linked with a change of hands, or change of direction, to wrong-foot the defence and get them out of position for the ensuing shot.

Outside the 'hole' there is still a chance to

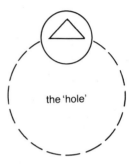

Fig 21   The best area to receive and shoot.

score on a longer shot and many attacks need to develop strength and speed of shot for this area of shooting. Indeed, it is not only so-called attacks who need shooting skills. Many times in a game a defence can see a channel of space to move into, either with the ball, or to receive it, and they should be equally adept at shooting.

The bounce shot from 5–10m out is a powerful overarm or side-arm shot which can create problems for goalkeepers. There are two points at which judgements have to be made. One as the ball is released, the other as it bounces. This is what makes the shot difficult to cover. Power is gained by moving the body weight into the shot and pulling hard with the bottom arm as the stick head pushes through. Sometimes a long high shot, safely placed to a top corner, can take defence and goalkeeper completely by surprise. Whilst they are still organising and positioning, a resourceful attack can shoot a goal.

Shooting is the exciting culmination of a series of events, perhaps a flurry round goal, a lost possession, a long series of

Fig 22   Using an extended stick to create space to receive and shoot.

accurate passes, an individual run or a set 'play'. The shot must be well chosen and calmly taken so that all previous efforts are rewarded. Practice and more practice by all team members could be the deciding factor in whether a team is able to take the split-second opportunities available to them in today's game to score that crucial goal.

COMBINATION SKILLS

There are several ways in which two attacks can combine the skills of carrying, sending and receiving to outwit their defences and create space for themselves. These can be practised as elements of play and can often be used within larger tactical situations.

Give and Go   (Figs 23–25)

This involves the sender in passing the ball off to another team-mate, sprinting round an opponent and immediately receiving the

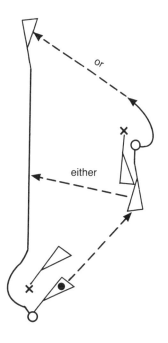

Fig 23   'Give and go'. Attack dodges to the blind side of the defence.

Fig 24(a)   The 'give and go'. A midfield player sends the ball to a connecting
cutter.

Fig 24(b)   The attack keeps momentum up and dodges on the blind side as the
defender watches the ball.

24

Fig 24(c)   The receiver returns the ball to the first attack who has sprinted ahead into space.

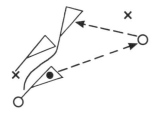

Fig 25   'Give and go' – attack moves ball-side and receives the ball close to the right ear.

ball again on the original line to goal. This combination is typically seen in the midfield, especially when a defence coming through can maintain momentum by passing off and receiving again in full flow. The move exploits the moment when opponents' eyes follow the pathway of the initial pass, allowing a fast-moving player the chance to sprint on into open space and receive again as a free player. (*Fig 23*).

Very often in the midfield the player moves to the blind side of her defender, away from the ball, once she has sent the pass. The opponent might have assumed the sender's job was over and is startled to find her sprinting on again to take the return pass. However, in less open situations, for example near goal, an attack might send the ball from her stick side and move towards the player who now has the ball. The stick can be protected and held at ear level, to the side, allowing a quick return pass followed, perhaps, by a shot at goal.

Attacking Skills

The person acting as receiver can be moving parallel or in an opposite direction to the original ball carrier. (*Figs 24 & 25*).

Scissors *(Figs 26 & 27)*

This is a move where the pathways of two players intersect diagonally. The player with the ball can move in front of or behind the other player. The intention is to make defenders adjust and change position because this is their moment of transition and weakness. The ball carrier can use this moment to exploit an opening just as the defences are deciding whether to switch opponents or stay with their own and crosse-over pathways. At this point the ball carrier may also pass and possibly sprint on to receive in a 'give and go' situation. This move can happen in various areas of the game but is

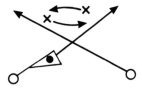

Fig 26   Scissors move to confuse the defence.

Fig 27(a)   The scissors move.

Fig 27(b)   Defence switching after the scissors move.

particularly useful when attacks are in a restricted area such as in front of goal or behind the goal crease. It can also be used midfield, for example after the draw when left attack may cut in to receive the draw and centre moves out to the wing to support if needed.

Stacking Manoeuvres   *(Figs 28–33)*

These happen when two players approach their defences in tandem formation, one behind the other and fairly close together. Traditionally, attacks have stayed well apart when defences marked closely one-on-one all the time, but now that defences co-operate more as a unit, working together to cover the shooting spaces, attacks must employ other ideas to create moments of indecision in the defence and exploit these moments to their advantage.

The ball carrier may be at the front or the rear of a stack with a variety of manoeuvres possible from each position. In situation (a) in *Fig 28* where the ball carrier is at the front of the stack, the defenders will be drawn together. The ball carrier runs straight at the pair of defences and then turns sharply, immediately before reaching them, dropping the stick head to protect it and facing her team-mate coming in behind. (*Fig 29*). This second attack now accelerates, driving hard to the side of the defences and receiving a little flicked-up 'dink' pass as she goes.

Alternatively, the front ball carrier O^1 may flick the ball behind to O^2 and screen the two defences slightly on one side as O^2 accelerates past her back on that side with the ball. Screening means that the attack places her body in such a position that the defence have difficulty moving across to the ball carrier. (*Fig 30*).

This move can also be started by the rear player carrying the ball in as O^1 screens. Another variation would be for the rear player to pass forwards and sideways to the

27

Attacking Skills

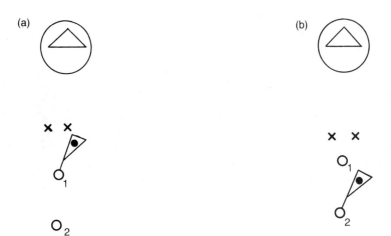

(a)

(b)

Fig 28   *Stacking-ball at the front or ball at the rear.*

front player who is moving away looking over her shoulder to receive. The pass is well protected and as O^1 drives hard having received the ball, O^2 cuts to the stick side for a 'give and go' beyond the defenders. (*Fig 31*).

Sometimes the front player can wait until she sees both defenders' attention is focused upon 'double teaming' the ball carrier, therefore ignoring her. As the defenders move to one side to take on the ball carrier, the front player can step out to the opposite side to receive the pass. The ball carrier must step back and away from the oncoming defences and give herself room to make the pass. (*Figs 32 & 33*).

When players are presented with the challenge of this arrangement they find numerous alternatives and possibilities within it. They need co-operation, spatial

Fig 29   *A stacking move where the ball carrier turns and protects the ball and passes to the trailing player.*

Fig 30(a) A stacking move where the attack
in front flips the ball to the side.

Fig 30(b) Having passed the ball the
attack in front blocks the pathway of the
defenders and the ball carrier
drives past on the protected side.

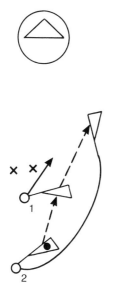

Fig 31 Screening for the 'give and go' move.

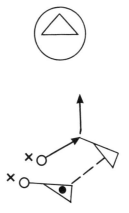

Fig 32 Using the 'double team' situation to
free an attack.

awareness, ability to accelerate at the right moment and flexibility of body and stick handling. This 2 v 2 situation gives excellent practice at 'reading' defenders' movements and reacting accordingly.

Setting a 'Pick' *(Fig 34)*

A 'pick' is the deliberate positioning of an attacker's body in the way of a defensive player thus causing the defender to have difficulty in staying with her opponent. In order to be safe, this must always be done in the visual field of that defender so that she has the opportunity to adjust her pathway. The ball carrier must run straight at her own team-mate (the pick) and at the last moment pass to one side, shoulders almost touching, so that the defender cannot find space to follow.

Fig 33(a)   The stacking move with the ball at the front.

Fig 33(b)   Passing the ball as the defence are drawn together.

If the ball carrier is being harassed by a defender on her left side, she will move past the pick, stepping to her right, and with her right hand high on the stick. If the defender is reaching from her right, the ball carrier will step to the left of the pick, with her left hand on the stick. (*Fig 34*) Attackers must move close to the shoulder of the pick, then drive away and accelerate to gain the advantage before the defenders can switch opponents. Picking for the ball carrier is a midfield move, whereas picking for the cutter is more likely in the critical shooting zone and is dealt with in Chapter 3, Team Attack.

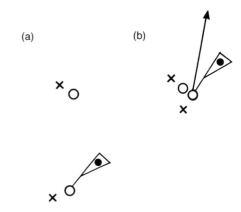

Fig 34(a) & (b)   Setting a 'pick' for a move to the right.

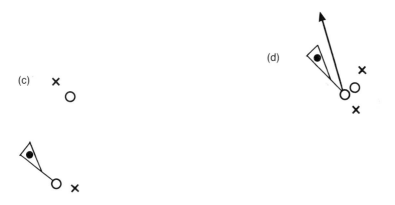

Fig 34(c) & (d)   Setting a 'pick' for a move to the left. N.B. In the midfield, the ball carrier must not use the pick if her defender is ahead. Only if she is level or chasing closely will she be able to see the pick and have a chance of repositioning.

2 Defending Skills

REGAINING POSSESSION

Possession is at its most vulnerable when the ball is released from the stick. Any bad pass or loose shot should be capitalised upon by an alert opponent. The whole team should be ready to intercept, block or be first onto the loose or out-of-bounds ball. Once the opposition has the ball, everyone in the team becomes a defence in order to regain possession at the earliest opportunity. Basically, a player playing man-to-man defence has to be aware of: 1. their own opponent, 2. the ball, 3. the opponent's goal. Awareness of all three is crucial from the beginning stages, and, as her game understanding develops, the defending player will start to realise which aspect has the greatest priority at which point in the game.

In general terms it is useful to give players the concept of a triangle to help their initial positioning as a defence. The three points of the triangle match the three elements mentioned above, and the defence moves within this triangle according to the defensive

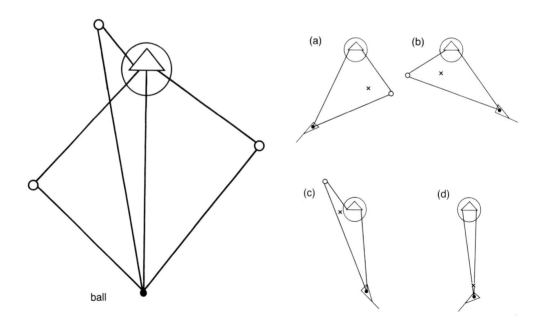

ball

Fig 35   Defensive triangles.

Fig 36   Positioning of the defence within the triangle.

problem, and the style of defence the team has chosen. (*Fig 35*). Each situation offers different problems to the defence, since their job is not just to mark their own player, but to be ready to help other defences, particularly the one whose player has the ball.

The diagrams in *Fig 36* show four different triangles that the defender might relate to in the game. In (a) and (b) the defender has not only to be prepared to prevent the ball being passed to her own opponent, but also to be ready to take on the original ball carrier if she gives her defence the slip. She must also be able to get goal-side of either attack should they have possession of the ball.

In *Fig 36(c)* the defender's own opponent is behind the goal and is not yet as dangerous as the ball carrier in front of goal. Positioning here relates mainly to the goal and the ball, but the defender must also cover the pathway which the attack behind the goal can take to come round the crease.

In *Fig 36(d)* the defender's own opponent has the ball so the focus here is directly on the ball carrier with the crucial reference point being the goal itself.

All the skills described below relate to this basic concept of the defensive triangle, and each gives a focus for the defence given the varying circumstances of the game. Coping with an opponent off the ball requires different skills from coping with the ball carrier. Individual skills must merge with unit skills so that each becomes a building block for whole-team defence.

In coping with an opponent who has not yet gained possession of the ball the defence needs to develop skills of:

1. interception,
2. reaching into the passing lane,
3. loose ball control,
4. out-of-bounds control.

They must also decide on their positioning generally within the triangle as the ball moves up the field and into the opponent's half. A defence can:

1. deny the pass,
2. concede the pass, but deny the pathway to goal,
3. take a position that gives them a chance to help out other defenders, if necessary,
4. slide from their opponent towards the ball carrier.

Obviously, a defender is constantly adapting and adjusting their off-the-ball position according to what their opponent is doing and how dangerous she is in relation to others in the opposing attack at that moment.

OFF-THE-BALL DEFENCE

Interception   *(Fig 37)*

Interception involves catching a ball that was meant for someone else. It is nearly always awkward in terms of distance, level and direction, and yet it requires acceleration onto, and away from, the situation. The stick is often extended for a one-handed catch or knock down. There must be a keen awareness of the position of the nearest opponent so that feet and stick can be pulled away from them and control maintained. Making an interception involves a risk, so think about safety first. Is the interception possible? How much danger is there if you fail? How far away from goal are you and can your defence help if things go wrong? All these questions require a player to assess the speed, direction, height of the ball, as well as the movement of their opponent.

Fig 37   Intercepting a pass to the attacker.

Fig 38   Reaching with the stick into the passing lane.

Practices

There are several simple practices to develop interception skills:

(a)   Stationary in twos: toss the ball above your head. Opponent reaches one-handed and attempts to control the ball and pull it away. Repeat on the run.
(b)   In threes: pass the ball between two players, the third player times her move to intercept and move away.
(c)   In two lines: feeder passes the ball to a connecting player. Interceptor runs on a diagonal to intercept and move away from tackle.

Reaching into the Passing Lane *(Fig 38)*

This can occur at either end of the passing chain when neither blocking nor intercepting

are possible. Sticks are extended into the most obvious passing lanes so that:

(a)   pressure is placed on the passer and receiver,
(b)   the pass may be knocked down,
(c)   the passer may choose a less direct line to goal,
(d)   it may force a poorer pass so that a team can intercept at a lower level on the field.

Attitude is very important here. Even if you are a few steps behind, or a few metres away, an extended stick can affect decisions made by the opposition, or at least make them aware of your presence.

Loose Ball Control   *(Fig 39)*

Statistically it has been shown that the ball is on the ground, or loose, a great deal. There

Figs 39(a)–(d)   By reaching one-handed for the ball the player is able to gain possession and protect the stick by changing the top hand and pulling to the left side away from the defender.

Fig 39(b)

Fig 39(c)

Fig 39(d)

is usually much pressure at this point. Players rush to the ball, which may be bouncing or rolling at odd angles. At this point the players must be mentally tough and ready to go for the ball. They need good footwork, speed and a variety of techniques to regain control of the ball. As players move for the ball they should consider whether they are goal-side of their opponent or whether there might be an opportunity for a shot once possession is gained.

It is not always possible to do the textbook pick up. Practise picking up with one hand on the stick, flicking or scooping the ball to a free team-mate, or pulling the ball quickly back or to the side whilst your opponent runs on. It is vital to concentrate on the ball since it can be moving in unpredictable ways and there is very little time available to execute the technique chosen. Keep the stick head still and focus its tip on the ball as you run. (*Fig 39*).

Out of Bounds

Here is a chance to regain possession. The ball is loose, so chase hard and get there first. This domination of the out-of-bounds situation will allow your team to start an attacking move. A positive attitude is crucial here. There are a number of decisions to be made:

● Can I get there first?
● Can I catch up and force a throw?
● Can I get close enough to put pressure on once play restarts?
● Have I no chance of getting the ball but need to position ready to cut off the line to goal?
● Have I other responsibilities that require me to stay back rather than chase for the out-of-bounds possession, e.g. being part of a zone?

This is one way of regaining possession that requires determination rather than technique. Get there first and you are given the ball. Easy! However, it is important to make the right decision initially and once possession is gained, it is important to move confidently out to where the umpire indicates, look around and have a positive stance ready for your next move. In other words, be ready to make the most of this advantage.

Denial Defence   (Figs 40 & 41)

This is the most positive and aggressive form of defence a team can use when marking man-to-man off the ball. It is based on the belief that it is better not to let your opponent receive the ball because, once she does, defending becomes much more difficult. Denial defence is physically and mentally very demanding, but to the trained eye, and for a good defence unit, it can be a rewarding way to play.

All the team must be fit and mentally tough, ready to work hard off the ball and, above all, never afraid to take risks. Each player must trust that others in her team are backing her up, and most important, are also playing to deny the pass.

Denial defence is most useful to gain dominance in the midfield. All coaches want connectors to cut towards the ball as it comes out from the clear, and indeed whenever there is pressure on the ball carrier. If defence wings and third man can deny the connecting pass and take away the passing lanes, then the flow and momentum of the opposing team starts to break down and there is the probability of a poor pass. It is vital that other players, usually attacks, put great pressure on the ball carrier. Otherwise your midfield defence will lose confidence and will start to worry about covering for fast breaks. The player with the ball will also be

Defending Skills

Fig 40(a)   Closed stance.

Fig 40(b)   More open stance.

Fig 41(a)   A connecting cut is blocked by denial defence.

Fig 41(b)   The attack rolls round into the space available behind.

Fig 41(c)   The attack cuts away at an angle having opened up a passing lane.

able to send a much more accurate pass if she is not under pressure.

Because a defence is committing herself more towards the ball-side, rather than goal-side, of her attack, denial defence is a high-risk activity and must be practised constantly as an individual skill. Although there is always the risk of an opponent exploiting the goal cut, it is difficult for the attack to free herself. It takes time and effort to shake you off. The ball carrier may not have that amount of time if she is pressured by her opponent.

The defender dictates the conditions under which she is willing to allow her attack player to receive the pass. Positioning is itself a confrontation which immediately sets the tone for the rest of the game. It is a good way to start a match since it gets each defender involved and feeling positive. However, it does need total commitment from all the defence and requires a sound

39

and equal level of ability and determination. Any weaknesses will soon be exploited.

Positioning is slightly to the side and in front of your player. Your stick is held across the passing lane and the front foot goes in front of the feet of your attack. The body is relaxed but ready with the knees bent, weight forward. (*Fig 40*). Vision of both player and ball is important and, at first, a more open stance may be easier thus opening up the field of vision. The most dangerous moment is when the attack finds the forward connecting cut is blocked and therefore rolls away to make a goal cut. (*Fig 41*). At this point the defence has purposely overcommitted to cut off the connecting pass and has left space behind. She must be ready to roll round and extend her stick across the passing lane. Even at this point a one-handed extension of the stick could be vital to knock the ball down or force her opponent to roll back up field. The pass required at this point is a difficult one, and a defence who is quick on the turn and uses good stick extension can still deny the pass or recover sufficiently even when the roll cut is successful. This is especially true midfield when the distance to goal is greater and a defender has time to catch up. Attacks often make flat cuts when the connecting cut is denied. These are caused by the initial position of the defence who has her front foot forward of the attack. The attack is tempted to move to her free side but this move is easy to cover with an extended stick. The move is also away from the ball but *not* towards the goal.

Conceding Defence *(Fig 42)*

This form of defence allows the connecting cut to occur but still requires defences to close mark and pressure the attacks. It means that the passing lane is open, but the

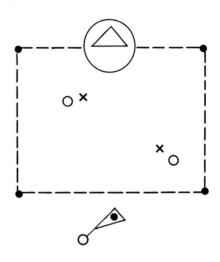

Fig 42   2 v 2 game with a feeder outside the square.

pathway to goal is closed down. This is a less aggressive, and somewhat less taxing, form of defence than denial, but nevertheless requires excellent footwork and determination. An alert defence can go for an interception if the pass is poor, or look to tackle as soon as the ball enters the stick. Positioning is constantly being adjusted so that the defence is ball-side and goal-side of her opponent. Again the defence triangle is a useful concept to help with positioning. A practice can be done with five players, 2 v 2 with a feeder. (*Fig 42*). This practice focuses the defence on their positioning. The feeder cannot shoot but can move round the square. Every time she moves, the defenders adjust their positioning in relation to the ball, the goal and their opponents.

Helping Defence *(Fig 43)*

If the attack manage to bring the ball into their half, each defender has to start adjusting her position in relation to the ball and the goal. (*Fig 43*). This position is based upon principles which develop the defensive triangle concept, as follows:

(a)   Every defence needs to keep ahead of the ball if they are to be of assistance to other defences later.

(b)   The ball carrier is the most dangerous player and must be closely marked. However, other defences need to adjust their position so that help can be given by double teaming. Here the defences are already alerting themselves to the ball carrier, the goal and their own attack.

(c)   The attacks who are nearest the ball tend to be the most dangerous and must be closely marked. Those furthest away from the ball are less dangerous though their path to goal must still be covered. Their defenders can drop in, towards the ball and

the goal, so that they can slide across more easily should an attack break through.

In *Fig 44(a)* X^1 is close marking the ball carrier. X^2 is one pass away and also close marking. X^3 knows that O^3 could only receive a long looping pass and therefore drops into a covering, helping position. She is also in a position to pick up O^3 should she cut in towards the ball and the goal. Notice the different positioning of each within the triangle drawn between the ball, their opponent and the goal.

If the ball is swung round to O^3 (*Fig 44b*) the positions and roles of the defence change. X^3 marks the ball carrier, X^1 runs back to keep ahead of the ball and towards the ball carrier. X^2 drops in towards the goal ready to help but also covering O^2's goal cut.

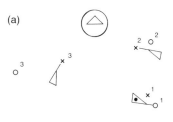

(a)

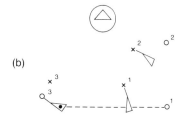

(b)

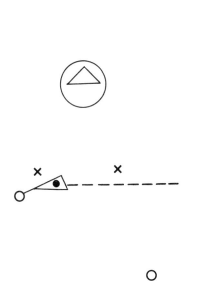

Fig 43   *Positioning of a helping defence.*

Fig 44(a)   *Defences positioning ready to help X^1.*
Fig 44(b)   *Defences repositioning ready to help X^3.*

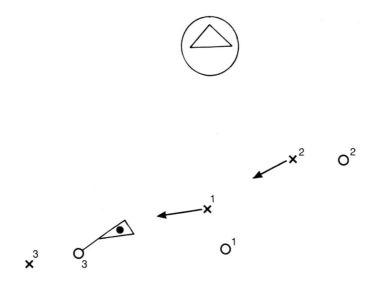

Fig 45   Defences sliding to cover the free attack O³.

Sliding   *(Figs 45 & 46)*

'Sliding' occurs when an attack gets past her own defence. The nearest defender slides across to challenge the free player. Timing and the angle of the slide are crucial. Too early and the pass is made easily to your attack. Too late and the ball carrier could be in a shooting position. This movement must be balanced, yet quick, so that any dodge or weave by the attack can be covered. The stick should be high to cover the passing lane to the free attack, but also ready to block the shot.

ON-THE-BALL DEFENCE

When an attack has possession of the ball their opponent can have a variety of intentions. These may be to:

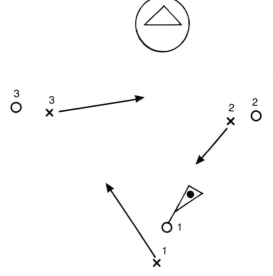

Fig 46   O¹ has beaten her defence; X² and X³ are equidistant; X² slides as she is on O¹'s strong upper hand side; X³ slides to O²; X¹ catches up to cover O³.

● Tackle the stick to dispossess.
● Block the ball as it leaves the stick.
● Slow down the ball carrier.
● Force the ball carrier to pass or shoot from their weaker side.
● Steer the ball carrier off their intended pathway to goal, or towards a helping defence.

Tackling *(Fig 47)*

This is a controlled tapping of the opponent's stick, either the stick head or the handle. This must be done safely so that body contact, roughness, or excessive force are avoided. A defence must ask herself the following questions before tackling:

● Where am I in relation to my opponent's stick?

● Where am I in relation to the goal?
● Am I ready to tackle?

To avoid body contact, tackling into the face, or other rough play, think about the positioning of the feet. (*Fig 47*). Some attacks do not protect the stick adequately. If they hang the stick head out, then tackle. This applies even when you are behind the player as long as the stick and the tackle are away from the body. Control, balance and safety are the key elements when considering whether or not a tackle is possible.

Decisions may alter depending on the situation. Tackling is a wholehearted commitment to regain possession. It must be successful otherwise a player can dodge and become a free player or shoot a goal. A defence must decide whether this movement of body and stick is valid given the circumstances. It may be safe to steer a

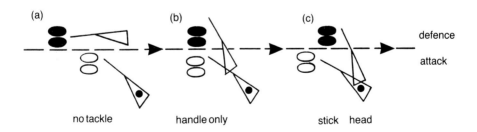

Fig 47   *Positioning of feet for a tackle.*

Defending Skills

player wide, slow them down, or pressure the pass. Ask yourself what the attack is able to do. Are they in a shooting position? If so, then you must tackle or concede the shot. Are they midfield but wide and outside the shooting zone? Is your defence unit spread and therefore vulnerable? If so, then perhaps it is not worth the risk of tackling just yet. Judge whether the attack is tempting the tackle. One lunge and a skilful attack has gone to goal.

The tackling motion on the stick head should be:

● Away from the body if possible, and particularly away from the head.
● A short, sharp 'rebound' motion to disturb the rhythm and dislodge the ball.
● A firm tapping, rather than a large swiping action, from a balanced base.

Sometimes tackling the stick head is difficult, or poses too much of a commitment in terms of body movement, whereas the stick handle, either between the hands or below the lower hand is available. This tackle should be short, sharp, and very accurate to avoid body contact. It can be very disconcerting and distracting to the attacker.

Blocking *(Fig 48)*

Blocking occurs as the ball leaves the sender's stick (whereas interception occurs as it arrives at the receiver's stick). It depends on players being aware of when and where the ball is likely to leave the opponent's stick. It requires close marking, good balance and control. The stick covers the pathway of the ball as it leaves the stick. Movements must be precise. It is not a large

Fig 48   Blocking the pass.

movement and is quite different from the action of a tackle. The position of the stick head can be either face or back towards the ball, depending on the situation. If a player is close marking, the stick head can be either back or face towards the ball for blocking, whereas a player moving across space to block a pass is more likely to open the face of the stick to the ball.

Slowing Down the Ball Carrier *(Fig 49)*

An attack who is able to gather up speed is likely to create a fast break. A defender needs to move in such a way that she places herself on the pathway she knows the attack would prefer. She has a right to be there, the attack must alter her pathway accordingly. The defender has given the attacker something to think about other than running to goal. There is now an obstacle. The defender must decide which side is the attacker's favoured side for a dodge. A right-hand-up player tends to favour her right side, so the defender could adjust her position both bodily and with her stick to 'encourage' the attack to move to the other side. If the stick is held forward, away from the body, then the attacker has to change her pathway earlier and the defender can adjust and move with her. A defender must always give the attacker time and space to adjust her speed and direction. *(Fig 49)*. Thus the slowing down action of a defence should be a movement that angles away from the attacker's pathway, rather than towards or across it. Having said this, however, many attackers do not adjust their pathway to avoid a defence and barge uncontrollably into them. Defenders should hold their ground, making sure that no movement of their stick or body goes towards the attack, but also being firm in their stance and their determination to slow

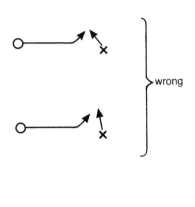

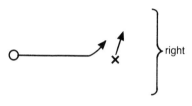

Fig 49   Slowing down the ball carrier.

the attack down. A defender has to practise changing from a body-checking stance which says 'stop' to the oncoming attacker, to a fast moving side-on run once the attack has committed herself to a pathway. This change can be improved by good balance and a ready position that is held on the toes, with the weight poised to go in either direction. The stick can be held out to balance the body as well as to slow the attacker down.

Forcing the Ball Carrier to Pass or Shoot from her Weaker Side

It is important that every defender assesses her opponent quickly at the beginning of the game. Most attacks have a preferred side even though they may have developed two-sided play. If the ball carrier is coming down the middle of the field her advantage will be considerably weakened if the defender forces her to move to her weaker side. The important thing then is to keep her on that side. Body positioning will do this and experienced defenders can often force a player to slow down and look around in frustration because she feels constricted and her initial speed has been dissipated.

Steering *(Fig 50)*

Steering is the movement of the defender once she has forced the attack to move off her intended pathway and, possibly, to move her stick to her weaker side. In this case the weaker side could mean the non-preferred hand of the attacker, or the side furthest away from the best line to goal. For example, a defender would be happy to steer a right-handed player towards the right wing since her pathway would be moving away from the best passing or shooting angle. A defender may decide to steer her opponent towards another defender so that they can double team the attacker.

Steering involves holding a strong 'barrier' position with the stick. By positioning body and stick across the chosen pathway, the defender effectively forces a different line to be taken if momentum is to be maintained. (*Fig 50*). Footwork has to be quick and often involves a cross-stepping action as the defender runs alongside the attacker. The key point here is never be drawn into an attempt to tackle. All concentration must be on maintaining the steering position. Clever attackers will tempt the defender by 'hanging out' the stick. Once the focus changes, the attacker can gain an inside line and go for goal. The defender must ignore all the signals and make herself wait for the attacker to run out of steam. This movement is used very often as an attack

Fig 50 *Steering an attack.*

runs down the wing and attempts to centre her pathway. It is also used when an attacker drives round the crease from behind the goal. A good steering position can take an attack away from a good shooting position, forcing a pass or a weak-angle shot.

Steering can be used to make an attack player move towards a second defender. This allows both defences to double team.

Double Teaming *(Figs 51 & 52)*

A double team involves two defences simultaneously putting pressure on the ball carrier. It is important, therefore, that each defence knows what their job is so that they do not negate each other's work, or commit a foul.

The defence assigned to the ball carrier usually becomes the primary defence who body checks, slows the attacker down and attempts to force a dodge to her weaker side. (*Fig 51*). The secondary defence player,

Fig 51 Double teaming an attack – defences both ahead of the ball carrier.

who moves to help the primary defender, goes to tackle the stick when it is pulled across, thus complementing rather than duplicating roles.

It is important that the primary defender concentrates on slowing down the attacker and does not reach across her body to attempt a stick check since this can often result in a foul. She must trust the secondary defender to finish the job. Good understanding of each other's roles is required here. Think 'body' or 'stick' and do the one task as well as you can.

This tactic is a high-risk activity because the second defence has had to leave her own player free. If she is lucky this may not be too much of a problem. For example, her opponent may be behind the ball, or may not have positioned herself well. However, if the ball carrier is driving to goal from outside the 8m mark, the second defence must release herself even if there is a high risk. This decision emphasises the principle that the ball is more important than the player, particularly in the critical shooting area. All defences should position themselves in anticipation of being the secondary defence in a double team.

A double team can be used anywhere on the field, though it is most commonly used in the critical scoring area around the goal. Obviously this is the point at which an attack with the ball is a potential scoring threat, and the shot must be pressured as much as possible.

In the midfield a double team can also be valuable to make the transition more difficult from defence to attack. (Fig 52). A chasing attack player can come from behind to take the stick check as the defender ahead slows the ball carrier down and forces her to take the stick behind her for protection. Players are often very unaware of the space behind them and can be caught out by a tenacious attacker.

Whenever a double team is being set up,

Fig 52   Double teaming an attack – one defence ahead, one behind.

the secondary defender must tell the primary defender that she is there, particularly if she is out of her vision. This knowledge will alter the way in which the primary defender positions, and will prevent her from feeling she has to go for a stick check.

The diagrams in *Figs 53–57* show different situations which defences can practise together. Remember to identify your own role and to communicate with each other. Good balance and control are vital here, since a mistake, particularly in the 8m area, can virtually give away a goal to the opposition.

Ball Carrier Driving from Behind Goal   *(Figs 53 & 54)*

As O^1 drives round, X^1 body checks and steers O^1 away from goal. However, if O^1 continues to come round the crease, X^2 must decide to leave O^2 and double team.

(Fig 53). This is a crucial decision since to leave O^2 is obviously risky. X^1 steers and keeps O^1 from moving into a shooting position. X^2 tackles the stick. Remember, if O^1 is steered well away from the crease, she becomes less dangerous and loses her shooting angle. In that case O^2 is in a more dangerous position and X^2 needs to cover her. This should be practised from both sides of the goal. If the ball carrier dodges inside X^1 onto the goal crease, then the goalkeeper becomes involved in the double team. *(Fig 54)*. The defences steer and the goalkeeper tackles the stick. This must be practised regularly so that the goalkeeper is not taken by surprise.

Ball Carrier Driving from in Front of Goal   *(Figs 55 & 56)*

This situation can be practised in different situations so that the defender practises

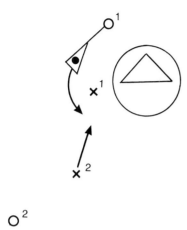

Fig 53 Double teaming an attack driving round the crease.

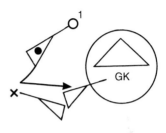

Fig 54 Goalkeeper involved in double teaming an attack.

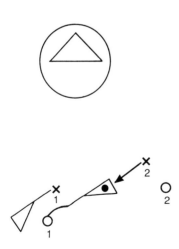

Fig 55 Double teaming in front of goal.

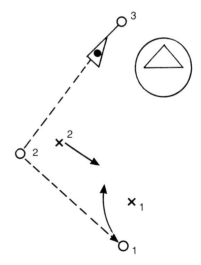

Fig 56 Practice for double teaming and defence positioning. O^1 drives to goal on receiving the ball. X^1 and X^2 double team.

Defending Skills

steering to her left or right depending on the position of the secondary defender. In each case X^1 is the steerer/bodychecker, X^2 tackles the stick. (*Fig 55*).

These simple 2 v 2 situations can be built up into larger units so that attackers have more choice and defenders more decisions to make.

In *Fig 56* the ball can start behind goal and move round the periphery to O^1 who drives between X^1 and X^2 (the right dodge is not 'allowed' in this practice since it is a defence practice for double teaming).

Later the attacks could choose whether O^1 or O^2 drives through the gap, and the defence can call their intentions to each other accordingly. Very often a verbal call will help defences learn their role and will give the coach some indication of any confusion. This practice can develop even further by adding a goalkeeper and X^3 to mark O^3. Now the attacks can choose which gap to drive through and defences can switch roles so that they have different problems to cope with.

Ball Carrier Coming through the Midfield *(Fig 57)*

In this situation the ball carrier is double teamed from in front and behind. An attacker chases back whilst the defender slows down the ball carrier. This can be practised in threes by starting play with the ball being

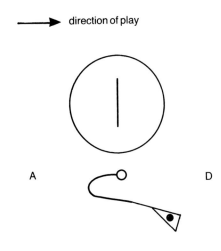

direction of play

A   D

Fig 57   Midfield opportunity for chasing attack (A) and defence (D) to double team.

rolled to O, the opponent, by the attack who is then going to chase as the secondary defender. O picks up the ball, pivots and runs to goal. A immediately chases whilst D starts to slow O down and steers her out away from her intended pathway. As O pulls her stick back to protect the ball, A should be in a position to tackle the stick. It is important that A does not move round into a body-checking position as the ball carrier slows down since she could block out or impede the more experienced and better positioned defender.

3 Set Pieces

The Draw *(Fig 58)*

The draw is the first chance a team has to gain possession. The position of the sticks, back to back at waist level with the ball held between, and the position of the foot up to, not on, the line, are standard features before the words 'Ready – Draw'. However, there are a variety of things a centre can do to attempt to gain control of the ball. These are variations of: timing, body position, force and direction.

Timing

No movement should occur before the word 'Draw'. It is important to note that the position the centres set into as the umpire checks the ball placement in the stick should not be altered as the umpire moves away. Some centres sink or adjust and thus can gain an unfair advantage. Remember, a movement of the sticks must be made by both centres up and away once the word 'Draw' is heard. However, this can be done immediately to get as early a draw as is legal, or sometimes a short pause may help to change the rhythm of the movement and gain an advantage. Care must be taken not to draw too soon or to stay still since both are fouls and will result in loss of possession. Centres should listen to an umpire's voice rhythm and watch her, if possible, to try to time the draw, but beware as some umpires purposely vary the timing of their command.

Fig 58 Setting up for the draw.

Body Position

The body is usually positioned with one foot forward up to the line and the other back with the hips lowered and knees bent to give good balance and explosive power for the action of the draw. It is best to place the body midway between the stick and the handle butt, to give good balance and control, but the position of the hands can be varied. Sometimes the lower hand is moved over the top of the handle with the wrist flexed so that the stick can be rotated under the ball on the word 'Draw'. This places the lower wood or plastic edge of the stick at an angle to the ball and can help control by tipping the ball onto the crosse.

Right-hand-up centres have long found the left-hand-up centre particularly difficult to beat on the draw. This is because the action is made towards the body rather than away when the upwards motion is begun, an action that is stronger and more compact. There is a disadvantage in that a left-hand draw position places the centre with her back towards the goal she is attacking. Nevertheless it may still be worth all centres practising left-hand-up since it changes the action and gives them a mechanical advantage.

Force and Direction

Some inexperienced centres use up considerable energy pushing their stick against that of their opponents in a great show of strength. Since nothing can happen until the umpire gives the command, save energy and concentrate on the extra force needed as the stick moves upwards to carry the ball to your team. Varying the force is a useful ability since players tend to position according to what has happened previously.

Centres who are able to send a long forceful draw right out to the wing, a short draw which can be taken within the circle, and a vertical draw which they can catch themselves, have a good armoury of possibilities. Remember also that if you have a tall, strong right defence wing who can get the draw and power through into attack, it may be advantageous to lose the draw by allowing the opposing centre to take the force of the action whilst you make a shadow move with very light tension.

Players around the Circle (Fig 59)

It is important that the two players in the area most likely to receive the draw, left attack wing and right defence wing, are quick off the mark and able to take the ball at full stretch with a strong wrapping movement of the stick head to take it away from other players' sticks. They must be very careful not to lose possession by moving into the circle too early, or by barging or impeding other players in any way with stick or body.

Third home is often involved in the draw, particularly if the centre can send a very strong high draw well outside the circle.

Having two players on the circle edge

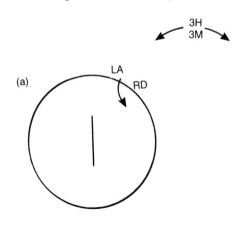
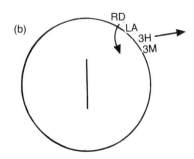

Fig 59   Possible positioning for the centre draw.

might also make life more difficult for the defences, but attacks must be aware of each other's roles and make sure they do not negate each other's moves. They should decide who is best to go for the short draw, who takes the high, looped ball, and so on. By gaining possession of the circle edge quickly after a goal, two attacks can make positioning difficult for the defences. Other players around the circle should also be aware of what is happening and how they can help after the draw has been made. For example, right attack might sprint fast down the wing to receive an early ball from centre or left attack if they gained possession. Alternatively, she may react quickly if the draw is lost and chase the opposing left attack to double team and regain possession.

The Throw

When a throw is taken you have an equal chance of gaining possession for your team. Everything must be done to maximise your chances. The rule states that you must be goal-side of your opponent and in all ways, sticks and bodies, no closer than 1m to your opponent. Having been positioned in this way by the umpire you must consider:

● Which side of my body is my opponent?
● What body position will suit me best, for example crouched or more upright, one foot forward?
● Shall I reach with both hands on the stick or do I need to reach one-handed? Is my wrist strong enough?
● Shall I change hands to give more stick extension from this position?
● Can I take the ball cleanly or will it be better to hook it out to the side for a team-mate or overhead ready for a quick turn to gain possession?
● Shall I wait and go for a stick check?

All these are individual decisions based on judgements about oneself and one's opponent. However, a player needs to look around and see who is near the area on her team and who could be a potential receiver of the ball. Once possession is gained the stick must be protected whilst the player goes towards goal or manoeuvres into a position to pass safely to a team-mate. Once the ball has been passed there is also a chance for a give and go, or a move to support the receiver as she moves into attack.

All these situations require speed off the mark, sound neat footwork to control the ball under pressure, and an awareness of team-mates and opponents. Wrist strength and the ability to catch and control the ball one-handed are important skills.

Readiness and speed off the mark must be controlled since moving too early can first result in a caution and then be followed by a free position to the opponent. This, of course, means a complete loss of possession for your team.

If a team-mate is involved in the throw then other players in the vicinity must be ready for the hook out or knock down situation. They must also be ready to go in for the ball immediately one of the players involved in the throw has touched the ball. This readiness could be either to help in attack, or to move quickly to defend should the throw be lost.

Free Position

When you are awarded a free position remember that you have been given full possession of the ball and you have a 4m space between you and your opponents. Use this opportunity carefully. Various options should be considered:

1. Am I near enough to shoot?

2. If I run with the ball could I then shoot, or draw a defence and enable another team-mate to shoot?

3. How many defences are there ahead? Could I take them on if I protect the stick head?

4. Is someone else open ahead in a better position than I am up the field?

5 Is there danger from behind, or to the side, once the signal 'Play' is given?

Free Position Shot on the 8m Mark

This free position, given when an offence occurs within the 8m area round goal, seems to be a wonderful opportunity for a certain goal. Remember, though, that you, as the person with the ball, are static and the goalkeeper has a clear unimpeded view of the shot. These disadvantages are added to by the fact that the nearest defences will be ready on the word 'Play' to move in as fast as they can to cover the shot.

There are two options: to shoot, or to pass. Shooting seems an obvious choice, but the shot must be well chosen. High shots from 8m are relatively easy to save. Look for a lower, non-stick-side area shot such as the bounce or skimming shot. Try to shield the stick head or change its level. Consider stepping forward or on a diagonal, if you think there is time. This might make the goalkeeper commit her body weight and then is the time to shoot.

The other alternative is not to shoot but to use the fact that defences are moving onto you to close down the shot. This could mean that a quick pass is on to a freer team-mate. It also means that the goalkeeper has to adjust her position. Defences covering this free position should think about covering different levels with their sticks. For example, the defence on the upper-hand-side could block the high stick head position. The nearest defence on the other side could cover the low shot with her stick head. Other defences could take the medium level. The position of all defences at this moment should prepare them for fast movement to the player on the word 'Play'. All players should practise this free position often since it is the only time a static shot can be taken and defended.

Out-of-bounds Ball

Dominating the out-of-bounds ball situation is critical in lacrosse since getting to the ball fast ensures team possession. All team members must be alert and fast off the mark to ensure that their team get to the ball first.

Having raced to make sure the umpire awards the ball to you, pick up the ball in your stick and march confidently into the field 4m, as is your right. With head up, weight forward and stick well protected you will tell everyone you are ready to attack.

This forceful, decisive attitude puts opponents on the defensive and gives your team an aura of confidence. Consider then whether to pass or run with the ball. Remember you are given 1m of clear space around you, enough to get a good pass forward, or protect the stick as you roll inwards to pass centrally. You could also take on your opponent and race through into attack.

If you know that you are beaten to the ball by an opponent, consider your positioning before play is stopped by the whistle. Get yourself goal-side and make sure you are covering the best passing lane.

Other players off the ball also need quickly to assess the situation so that they too are well positioned for the next stage after play resumes. Depending on who will be given the ball, other team-mates should ensure they are not out of position on the whistle.

4 Goalkeeping

A goalkeeper has an exciting and demanding role which requires tremendous concentration and consistency. The game may be at the other end of the field for long periods of time and suddenly she finds herself having to face a ball that could be the winning shot. A goalkeeper must therefore be totally involved in the game at all times, so that on all occasions she feels confident to save the shot no matter how little play she has had previously.

This position requires a certain mental toughness to play really well. A goalkeeper cannot dwell on past mistakes and it is her psychological strength which shows in her physical demeanour and in the way she talks to her defence. A good goalkeeper makes the defence unit feel safe and well supported. They, in turn, feel more able to do their own job rather than protect the goalkeeper. A confident goalkeeper appears to fill the goal space and makes attacks think twice about shooting.

Goalkeepers seem to fall into two main categories: positional and reaction.

The positional goalkeeper is often more consistent and works on moving to cover space and being in the right place at the right time. Often moving to the right position will save, or even prevent, the shot.

The reaction goalkeeper can do some spectacular saves but can also at times be out of touch. They are usually the risk takers and often have a pugnacious temperament. However, they are more likely to be beaten by a fake move or shot.

A goalkeeper should be willing to work long hours on both mental and physical skills. This position should never be given to the weakest player, but rather to one of the best players, since all the qualities required of a field player, such as quick reactions, good stick skills, ability to read the game, concentration and accuracy, are all required by the player in goal.

The kind of hand–eye co-ordination needed to play racket sports is required by a goalkeeper. The ball travels at its fastest during the shooting action and she has to

Fig 60 The goalkeeper comes out of her circle to help to clear the ball.

adjust both to the movement of the ball and the player. In lacrosse the task of goalkeeping is made even more difficult by the use of the space behind the goal. It is inevitable that, as the ball moves from behind to in front, the goalkeeper will lose sight of it. There are also moments when a goalkeeper can lose sight of the ball in front of goal because it is screened, either by her defences, or by attacks moving in relation to the ball. The ability to track and sight the ball quickly and adjust position accordingly is vital.

Equipment for the goalkeeper should protect, but not impede the necessary agility required by this position. Experimentation by goalkeepers is recommended so that they find the right combination for them within the parameters of the rules and of safety.

The most vulnerable areas for a goalkeeper are the head, throat and fingers. It is recommended that all goalkeepers should wear a full helmet since a face mask leaves the head unprotected. The helmet should provide good vision and fit snugly. A throat protector is rarely seen in the women's game but is used in the men's game to protect a very vulnerable area. It is particularly important for rising shots, such as a high bounce or underarm, and should be provided for all goalkeepers.

Gloves should be padded, within the limits allowed by the rules. Many goalkeepers save with the hands on the non-stick side (though the use of the stick is advised where possible) and should make sure that the palm is well padded. The way the stick is held will expose certain parts of the hands more than others, and goalies should choose gloves appropriate to their technique.

Chest, arm and leg protection has either been cumbersome or non-existent in the women's game and it is heartening to see lighter but stronger materials available for goalkeepers in all sports. It is useful to look around at other sports, such as hockey or American football, as well as the men's game of lacrosse to find combinations of protection to suit the goalkeeper in the women's game. Whatever is chosen, it is important that a goalkeeper looks just as active and agile as anyone else. A track suit or sweat shirt in team colours worn over the padding can make a big difference. Smaller fitted leg pads that fit under rather than over sweat pants can add to agility, though they obviously do not give as much cover for the low or bounce shot.

The stick should be as big as possible, within the existing rules of the game, and should be the first line of defence. At present a five, rather than four, leather wooden stick up to 9in wide is legal internationally, and in some areas the men's goalie stick is allowed in nationally agreed rules.

Whatever the present rule structure, it is important that a goalkeeper is dressed so that she is safe and warm. No one will be encouraged to play this position unless they see it as an enjoyable position to play, and one that is conscientiously coached and introduced to everyone beginning the game. Too often the position is neglected or only one person is introduced to the skills involved. Goalkeeping can be great fun for everyone to learn as basic grounding in the skills of the game, with opportunities then for those with special interest and aptitude to continue. It is also vital that goalkeepers play in the field to keep their movement and stick skills sharp and to develop understanding of attack and defence play. Over specialisation at too early a stage restricts the potential of any team player.

Movement and Stick Positioning *(Figs 61–66)*

One of the first things a goalkeeper should learn is how to position to cover the space in goal. Sliding steps are taken along an arc from post to post and this movement should be continually practised so that the goalkeeper knows, without looking or feeling with the stick, where she is in relation to the posts. One simple aid to help this is to mark a centre point at the front of the crease and then mark the arc. *(Fig 61)*.

Positioning on the arc depends on where the ball is, the aim being to cut down the shooting space available, first by facing the ball at all times, and second by moving forwards onto the arc and off the goal line to decrease the shooting angle and fill the goal. *(Fig 62)*. By positioning correctly, a goalkeeper can cover many of the angles available to the shooter. Remember that it is vital to relate to the ball in the stick and not to the body of the attack. *(Fig 63)*. This is an important point since attacks use both stick extension and change of hands which can considerably affect the direction of the shot, even when the body is in virtually the same position relative to the goal. Some goalkeepers tend to position so that they leave

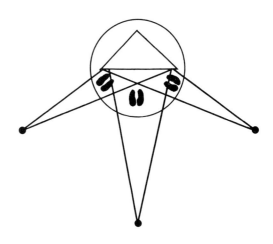

Fig 62   Covering the shooting angle.

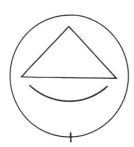

Fig 61   The arc and midpoint mark.

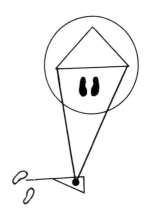

Fig 63   Position to the ball not the player.

more of a gap on their stick side, thus tempting the attack to place the ball on that side, since the weakest points for a goalkeeper are on the non-stick side, particularly about waist level.

All shots should be stopped from a ready or set position. (*Fig 64*). The body should be balanced and steady, with the weight forwards over the toes, and feet slightly apart. The stick is held forward of the body with the hands apart. The height of the head of the stick depends on the distance the ball is from the goal. The stick moves higher and nearer the ear as the ball gets closer. It is held at mid-level, ready to drop low for a low or bounce shot or lift up for a high shot, when the ball is further away. The top hand can be placed with knuckles in front or behind the stick, but the elbows should be relaxed and

outside the line of the stick. The face of the stick should be used to cover space and to help create an impenetrable shield. The stick head should mirror the height of the shooter's stick and should be held in such a way that it can be moved quickly to the non-stick side to block a high shot or sweep low to block a low or mid-level shot. (*Fig 65*).

From the set position all movement should be out and slightly across to block the shot. Crossing the feet should be avoided as should any 'wrapping' movement of the stick. Both mean the body is unbalanced and moving laterally across the flight of the ball. The leading foot should match the side to which the shot is directed. A shot to the right-hand space should be met by the right foot, with the trailing foot following immediately. A shot to the left-hand space should

Fig 64   Goalkeeper's set position.

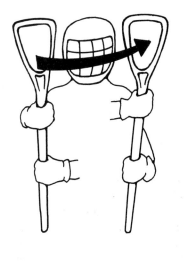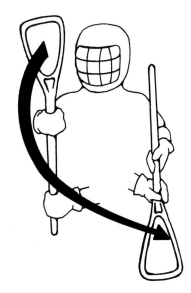

Fig 65   Moving the stick to the non-stick side.

Fig 66   Goalkeeper saving a low shot.

be met by the left foot. The technique of stepping out to the ball should be practised continually, sometimes without a stick and using soft practice balls to show the goal-keeper the importance of correct body position. Stepping to the ball decreases the angle and puts the body behind the flight of the ball. (*Fig 66*).

It is important to stress three aspects of goalkeeping:

1.   Moving round the arc to cover the position of the ball with stick and body.
2.   Setting and balancing as the shot is being prepared, matching stick with stick.
3.   Reaching to the released ball and stepping to the shot.
Often the second aspect is missed out and the goalkeeper is still moving sideways as the ball is released. It is important to be balanced and able to move forward as the ball is released.

Saving the Ball *(Figs 67–73)*

A save occurs when the ball is *stopped* or *blocked*, not necessarily caught, by the goalkeeper. The save itself should be made with the stick held forward and in front of the body. The arms extend the stick to the ball so that when the ball enters the stick the force can be absorbed by going back with the top arm. (*Fig 67*). A wrapping action should be avoided since there is a danger of mistiming the movement or of flicking the ball off the stick into the goal. This basic extension of the stick and 'give' behind the shot is basic to any save but the position of the head of the stick will alter according to the shot. Moving the stick to the non-stick side is the hardest. It must move in the most direct line, keeping the head of the stick facing the ball.

Obviously rebounds must be avoided where possible since they give an attack a second chance, but undue emphasis on the traditional catching action is inappropriate when trying to stop an extremely hard shot.

There are two lines of defence: the stick and the body. Correct positioning will give immediate results since the shooting angles are covered and the shooter has to make the shot. Make sure that a goalkeeper knows when a shooting angle starts to appear; many goalkeepers move unnecessarily when a player has the ball at the side of the goal. A goalkeeper has to learn the discipline of 'holding the post' (*Fig 68*), that is positioning in an upright stance, with shoulder against the near post, stick held high to cover the space by the head and weight poised to start moving only when a shooting angle appears. (*Fig 69*). A goal scored on the near-side post has been *given* by the goalkeeper not *taken* by the shooter.

The nearer the ball comes to the crease, the higher the stance and stick position should be. (*Fig 70*). The running line of the attack should be carefully considered. If the attack runs across the goal, the goalkeeper should stay on her arc following the ball (*Fig 71*), only moving out once the ball is released. If the attack is moving straight towards the goal the goalkeeper must judge

Fig 67   *Saving a high shot.*

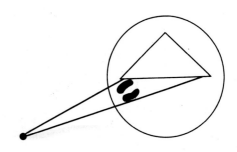

Fig 68   *No angle. Hold the post.*

at which point she should move off the arc to narrow the angle and possibly, if the shooter gets very close, to smother the shot (*Fig 72*) which will very often at this point be high to avoid a crosse-over.

The low or bounce shots bring specific problems of their own. The low shot is

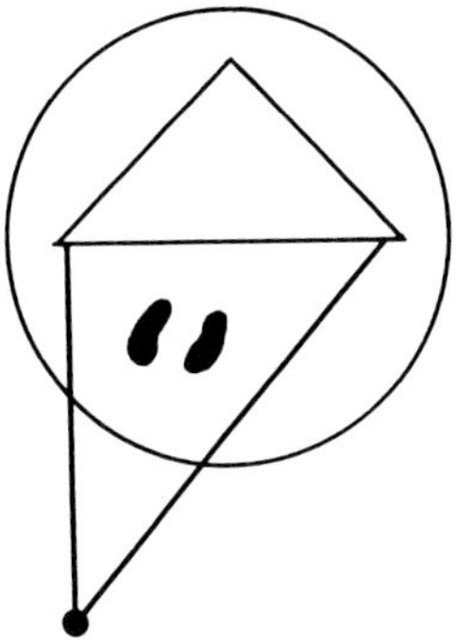

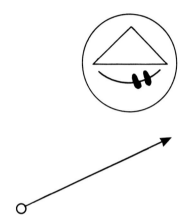

Fig 69 Angle appears. Goalkeeper must shift position.

Fig 71 Move on the arc to cover the cutter moving across the goal.

Fig 70 Positioning for a close high shot.

Fig 72 Move off the arc to smother the shot if the attack drives to the crease.

covered by the stick being held low and following the ball. Leg pads are useful back-ups for these shots. The stick-side low shot can be very fast and requires little prepara-tion. The underarm is more obvious but can sometimes be screened until the last moment. In both cases body and stick position are important and the marking defence must try not to block the goal-keeper's vision in their attempts to prevent the shot.

The more difficult shot is the bounce shot since there are two problems with which to contend. First, the release of the ball must be watched and, second, the bounce itself, which can be problematic because of ground conditions that may cause the ball to skid or kick or change line. Always step to the ball and keep the pads square to the shot. Sometimes it is possible to reach the ball before it bounces but, if not, then the

Fig 73 Saving a bounce shot.

head and weight should be over the ball to absorb and block a high bounce. (*Fig 73*). Concentrate on watching the ball and keep-ing the mask parallel to the ground. This protects the throat and keeps the weight forward. The stick should be held with the stick head down and the handle in front of the body. The lower hand should slide up the handle so that the stick can be adjusted upwards if necessary.

Blocking the Shot

There will always be a moment when it is better to take on the shooter rather than hold position in goal. This is a crucial decision to make and experience helps as well as prac-tice. However, if the attack is running straight to goal or has received the ball close to goal in a relatively static position, it may be advantageous to rush the shooter and perhaps surprise her. Another example is when a player comes round the crease and gets on the crease side of her defence. The goalkeeper may be better double team-ing rather than waiting on her post. This is a very important decision and a mistake can be fatal. For example, the goalkeeper might move out too early and allow the attack softly to lob the ball over, or may move too far and take the ball on her pads outside the crease which is, of course, a foul. However, this move can also be successful and shows determination and attack by the goalkeep-er. Very often it is better to keep one hand only on the stick to allow the stick head to move up and over the shooter's stick whilst the other hand balances the goalkeeper.

When a player is moving round the crease it is important to judge whether she is mov-ing on a good line to get a shot or is actually fading off upfield. If the player is driving round towards the goal, the goalkeeper must step towards the edge of the crease; if the player fades away then she must set and wait on the arc for any shot to be made.

Playing the Ball behind the Crease

When the ball is taken behind the goal, the goalie should stand directly in the centre of the cage, about 1m from the goal line, facing the back of the goal. In this position she is ready to take one step and be on either post. If this position is consistent, she will turn to the post more accurately. When she turns she should follow the ball and turn *into* the post. She should take the left leg to the left post first, when she turns, and the right leg to the right post. This means that she gets square to the shot quicker. When the ball is behind the goal the goalie should be constantly assessing the situation. This means thinking about whether the feeder is more dangerous than the player in front of goal or vice versa. It also means assessing what the attack are trying to do when the ball is behind goal.

The goalkeeper holds her stick in a position ready to intercept passes. She may be afraid of deflecting a pass into the cage but should be encouraged to be positive and try to intercept. One thing that must be avoided however is lunging, or jumping to catch the pass, thereby losing balance and being unable to turn and set for the shot if the interception is missed.

After the Save

Once the ball has entered the crease the goalkeeper has ten seconds to clear the ball. She should quickly decide whether to pass immediately, just as the attack perhaps slump or lose concentration, or whether to hold for a few seconds whilst the defence organise themselves. Clearing the ball accurately for a short or long clear is a skill needing constant attention as there is nothing worse than a good save ruined by an incompetent clear. The long clear will need a slipped top hand to add extra leverage and a good strong step into the throw to transfer weight into it. The follow through also needs to be exaggerated with the larger-headed sticks.

Clears should usually go to the outside of the field for safety. A clear up the centre of the field should be made to a free player moving towards the ball, if it is to be safe.

Outside the Goal

A goalkeeper should have excellent picking-up skills for fielding a loose ball behind the goal. She should also be able to pass accurately when under pressure and should practise taking part in a throw situation. Playing outside the goal-circle should be encouraged as it adds to the excitement and involvement of the role. Deciding when to move out and when to stay in goal is a vital skill for a goalkeeper.

Talking to the Defence

A goalkeeper is an important element in the defence unit. She is able to watch the game and can warn the defence about the position of the ball and about other dangerous players other than their own opponent. She should practise telling the defence where the ball is, 'Ball behind', 'Ball right', etc. and also alert the defence to free players: 'Cutter right', 'Watch the centre'.

In the men's game the goalkeeper has a much more central role as defence organiser than in the women's game. However, good goalkeepers have always communicated well with their defence, keeping them united and working smoothly together.

Coaching the Goalkeeper

The goalkeeper should receive logical and regular coaching. Points to consider are:

1. Never allow shooting practice by attacks without a defence. This can be intimidating and counter-productive.
2. Assign someone to help warm up the goalkeeper before practice and matches whom she trusts and who will shoot accurately and safely.
3. Plan a logical build up for practices and warm-up that increases in difficulty.
4. Allow the goalkeeper time on the field as well as in goal.
5. Discuss what kind of warm-ups help her and how long it needs to be.

Warming up the goalkeeper should be planned so that simple shots progress to more difficult shots. For example, a stationary shot is easier to save than a shot taken on the move. Shots from a distance are easier than those taken close to the crease.

This is an example of how a warm-up could progress:

(a) Start with shots from the side about 8m from the goal and move in to the middle. Aim in a logical way, perhaps dividing the goal into squares (*Fig 74*) remembering that the non-stick side saves are more difficult to cope with. If two people can warm the goalkeeper up, the practice goes quicker and there is movement round the arc from side to side. The ball can also be passed across before the shot is taken.
(b) Shoot after running across and then at an angle. This can develop into running down to the goal.
(c) Feed from behind so that the goalkeeper can practise moving to cover the feed then the shot.

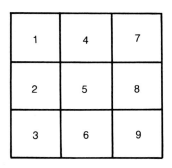

Fig 74   Divide the goal into sections for goalkeeping practice.

(d) Drive round the crease to show movement to the post and then out to block, or onto the arc, depending on the angle.
(e) Practice could then include 1 v 1 and 2 v 2 since it is important that the goalkeeper and the defence unit work together.

Practices

All the above warm-up activities can be practised separately to develop particular areas of work. Here are some other practices to help the goalkeeper:

1. Using a soft ball for shooting, play with an old stick with the gut and leathers cut out, to practise correct body positioning.
2. Use a soft ball, or place the goalkeeper behind wire netting, and send the ball at her mask. Work on keeping the eyes open and not shying away from the ball.
3. Place soft weights on the ankles while practising to put emphasis on quick, agile footwork. This is equivalent to running with weights to increase stamina.
4. Practise with more padding than is worn in the game. Repetitive practices can be distressing if the goalkeeper finishes with more bruises than successes.
5. Learn the dimensions of the goal by

closing your eyes and (a) moving round the arc from post to post, and (b) touching the four corners of the goal with the stick head with eyes closed.

6. Improve reactions by throwing a ball against a wall and saving the rebound, *or* get a player to throw from behind you at a wall so that you can take the rebound.

7. Practise out-of-goal skills like picking up and passing on the run.

8. Play lacrosse on the field to improve speed and game knowledge. Play other games, such as squash, which demand speed and good reflexes.

Remember that goalkeeping, perhaps more than any other position on the field, requires confidence, the ability to read the game, good rapport with team-mates in defence and excellent concentration. Practice alone and with her team, attack and defence, is vital to keep the goalkeeper's skills tuned and to keep her motivated and determined to improve.

5 Team Attack

When talking about teams working together in attack and defence it is important to stress that, once possession is gained, everyone is an attack, whereas the converse is true when possession is lost.

Think of the field as a whole when attacking or defending rather than as a 'defence half' and an 'attack half'. The field can be divided into three *zones* each requiring different roles when players find themselves there. Every player should know what to do in any part of the game since it is unrealistic to believe that homes only shoot goals and straight defences only defend the goal.

The three zones (*Fig 75*) can be identified as:

● The *clearing zone* – where the ball is being cleared away from the goal.
● The *transition zone* – where the ball is being carried through the midfield.
● The *critical shooting zone* – where the ball is at or near a point from which a shot can be taken.

In this chapter and the next the possibilities for attacking and defending within these zones are explored.

THE CLEARING ZONE

Once a team gains possession of the ball each member has a part to play in the sequence of attack progression. Every player from the goalkeeper forwards must know her contribution to the attacking pattern. All team members that find themselves in their clearing zone at the point of possession know that the first essential is to move the ball out sideways away from the critical shooting area or 'hole'. (*Fig 76*).

Clearing Pattern *(Figs 77 & 78)*

Players should become aware of the field in distinct lanes – a central channel and two side channels. (*Fig 77*). The first pass will be a 'going-away' pass, the receiver already having good forward momentum and pace, to the outside lanes.

Receivers should ask with the stick to the

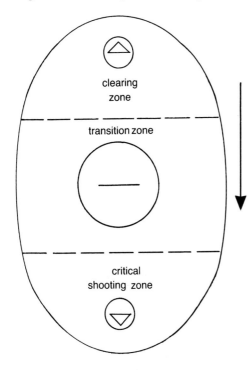

Fig 75   Field of play.

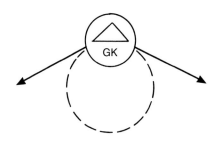

Fig 76   *Clearing areas away from the 'hole'.*

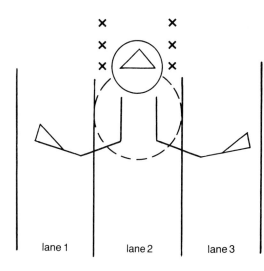

Fig 77   *Clearing lanes.*

outside of the game, with over-the-shoulder eye contact, keeping the target still and out, to present good visibility for the goal-keeper's firm, flat clearing pass. Players should quickly become aware that to leave the 'hole' uncovered is potential suicide and, as the attacking movement is flowing upfield, someone must be ready to cover the middle in case of a sudden change of possession.

If a central player is introduced they learn to assume specific roles from the beginning. A and B (*Fig 78*) both cut out for the first pass. The pass went to A who, having received, looked immediately inwards for the next pass. It is vital to bring the ball back into the central channel as soon as possible as this opens up attacking options upfield. C is the central cutter who 'motors' up the central channel looking for the next pass and B, who was not used for the clear, rolls back into the middle and covers the centre, backing up the first cutter or becoming a receiver if necessary. It is a good idea to encourage players to state verbally what their job is as they are doing it, to reinforce and clarify their position, so that in this example B will call, 'Covering the middle'.

Once players appreciate this basic concept they can be introduced to depth of choice in the clear and new roles to play. Goalkeepers should have the choice of clearing out a short clear to either side or a long clear to either side channel, i.e. four cutters all expecting the ball and when one is selected the other three have specific jobs to do.

If the ball goes long to D, the same-side short cutter A moves behind D, the receiver, calling, 'Supporting ball'. She should be positioned to help out and sweep up any fumbles or poor clears.

Opposite-side short cutter B turns back as safety, calling, 'Covering the middle', and

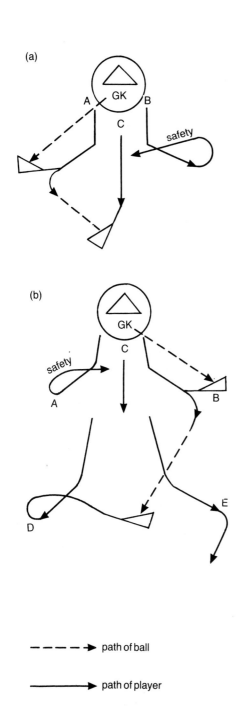

(a)

safety

(b)

safety

--- --- ➤ path of ball

─────────➤ path of player

Fig 78   Building up a clearing pattern.

opposite-side long cutter E turns inside and cuts as the next potential receiver.

If the clear goes short to B, the other short cutter, A, turns back and covers the middle, playing safety. Opposite-side long cutter D cuts back to the centre and down the middle for the pass, and the cutter ahead on same side, E, cuts out first and then back to help.

Having brought the ball safely through the clearing zone the attacking momentum is now in transition.

THE TRANSITION ZONE

Successful clearing combinations will have brought the ball well up through the midfield, probably in the central channel, from which many more attacking options are possible.

The attacking team's first consideration will be to look for the possibility of a fast, incisive early ball forward, thus gaining the chance of creating a free player driving towards goal, having left her defence behind. The team is now in a classic 'fast break' situation where they outnumber the opposition by at least one player in their attacking 'play'. All players need to know the best combination of spacing and moves and be able to read the situation and position accordingly.

Fast Break – the 'L' Play   *(Fig 79)*

(a)   The ball carrier (O^1) should be ahead of her defence and driving hard on goal, positioning herself slightly to one side of the central channel on the field.

(b)   The next attack up the field (O^2) must draw to the opposite side of the channel, parallel to O^1 and be ready to receive a square pass from her. (O^2's defence will

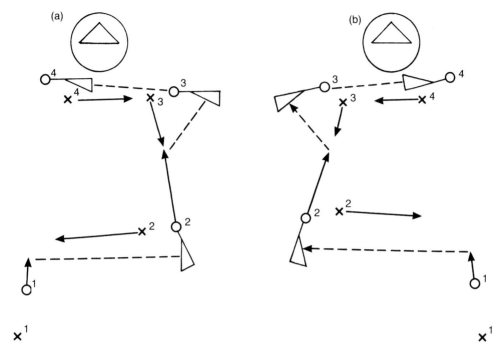

Fig 79   The fast break.

initially mark her forward movement but then be forced to take the greater danger of a free ball carrier.) O^1 will give the ball as the defence is coming onto her, making sure the pass is square and not forward as this can be easily blocked or intercepted.

(c) O^2 must pass to O^3 on the outside of the field.

(d) O^4 may need to move across and away from the goal mouth to enable a safer pass from O^3 and to get a better shooting angle.

All passing should be flat, fast, direct and without delay to prevent the defence ahead reorganising and before chasing midfielders have a chance to catch up.

Alternatives

If the fast break is not possible, ball carriers coming out of the clearing zone need players ahead of them to be presenting alternative possibilities to ensure safe, team posses-sion. As the ball is arriving in the transition zone, players ahead should already be *making space* (see page 11) so that they can cut decisively at the right moment to receive the ball. These forward connecting cuts (*Fig 80a*) are vital if a team is to domi-nate the midfield. (*See Fig 6.*) If a player has made a connecting move forward to meet the ball carrier and not been used it is essential that she works again to be a poten-tial receiver by then making a goal cut. (*Fig 80b*). Here the player rolls back and asks for the pass, moving away from the ball carrier and towards the goal. (*See Fig 41c*). Players must remain positive and decisive in their moves and not let them deteriorate into flat cross cuts which are vulnerable and very easy to defend. It is essential that midfield-ers read the game situation as it moves upfield and get themselves up ahead early so that they can then come back down to make the connection with the clearing ball carrier.

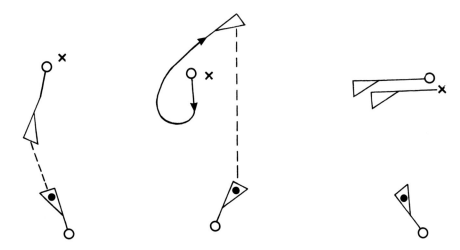

Fig 80(a) The connecting cut.   *Fig 80(b) The goal cut.*   *Fig 80(c) The 'flat' cut should be avoided.*

Fig 80 Cutting.

Another alternative to making space for connecting moves and then goal cuts is to assess one's position relative to the ball, and to *move out*, if appropriate, thus opening up space for other players to use.

Combination Plays

As the ball is moving through the transition zone this is an ideal time for combination plays with other team-mates to force moments of indecision in the defence and create an overlap for the attacking team.

Give and Go

Passing the ball off then accelerating to receive it again, moving behind or in front of one's opponent, is an excellent way to get ahead, keep the forward speed and momentum going and create a one-up situation. It is also a good idea for a free ball carrier entering the transition zone to look for the 'give and go'. This forces the defences' attention to switch focus and prevents them homing-in on a fixed carrying point and adjusting as the ball approaches.

Scissors

The old obsession for spreading out and splitting the defence as the major attacking strategy for a team can only be a partial answer in the modern game. The defence know now that: (a) there is strength in numbers, (b) they must never get themselves isolated, (c) the ball carrier is the most important threat. Any self-respecting defence will no longer be drawn wildly out of position, so attacks who move closer together can, as a pair, wrong-foot defences, force them into moments of indecision and even cut off their space. Scissors moves or crossing pathways create possibilities as do the following manoeuvres.

Stacking Manoeuvres

There are a multitude of arrangements possible when players relate to each other in tandem, one behind the other.

Setting a Pick

In the transition zone, setting a pick for the ball carrier can relieve her from a pressurising defender and create a clear pathway to drive forward and cause problems for defenders ahead. Eye contact, a non-signalling stick, and only a medium-pace approach, are all cues for the ball carrier to use the player ahead as a pick rather than a connector.

Trailing

If the ball carrier has overtaken team-mates connecting to the ball, these players must then double back and assume a 'trailing' position to support the ball and be an alternative receiver if the ball carrier runs into trouble ahead. It is advisable for her to call 'Trailing' to inform the player ahead as she moves in behind.

Team Flow in Transition

We have dealt with both individual work and combination plays in the midfield but members must be ready as a whole team to adapt to situations, or suddenly change the play to unbalance the opposition and gain the advantage.

Change the Pace

Although high-speed progression of the ball through the midfield is something looked for initially, ensuring safe team possession is far more important. It may be just as advan-

tageous in the long run to slow the pace of play down in the middle of the field and then dramatically speed it up as the attacking momentum reaches the critical shooting area. This can really take a defence unit by surprise and create the necessary openings.

Swing the Ball *(Fig 81)*

If the attacking team is progressing down the side of the field, the long swinging pass from one wing across to the other can open up spaces and force all members of the defensive unit to reposition and adjust. As the defences' eyes follow the ball across the field and they begin to change their role in the unit, cutters on that feeding side must utilise the moment of transition. They may arc in towards the goal on the blind side of their defender in the 'back-door space'. *(Fig 81)*.

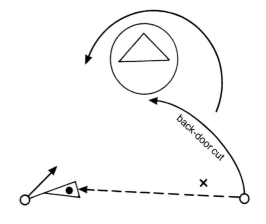

Fig 81   Moving blind-side of the defender.

Team Attack

Other cutters may go on behind the goal and come round to cut for the new receiver.

Move into the Centre

Attacking teams should aim wherever possible to bring the ball into the central channel of the field as they move from the transition zone into the critical shooting area. This gives the team many more options for play to both sides, making defending much more difficult for the opposition.

Rebuilding the Attack after Pressure *(Fig 82)*

When a team is under intense pressure in the defence it may be necessary for all team members to be back deep in their clearing zone, helping out. However, a team should try to leave one or two members high up the field in readiness for a change of possession. When this moment arrives, the defender streaming out with the ball often finds she has overtaken most of her team before she has progressed very far. Everyone needs to be aware of the problems and possibilities this presents and be ready to move quickly to capitalise on the large spaces now available.

The two remaining attacks waiting upfield now become the connectors and drive down to meet the ball carrier while the attacks, who were down in defence, turn and sprint on the outside of the field to support the forward movement and become potential receivers nearer the goal. It is important for those on the outside of the field to keep out so that the central channel remains clear, leaving the middle attack to support the connector from behind. (*Fig 82*).

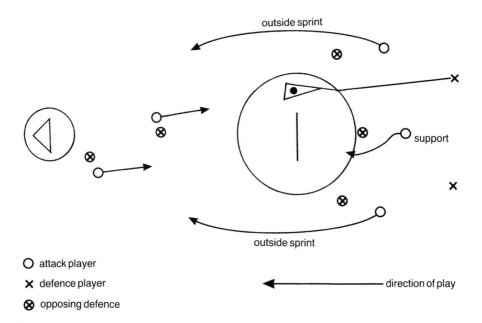

outside sprint

support

outside sprint

○ attack player

✗ defence player

⊗ opposing defence

⟵ direction of play

Fig 82   Building up the attack through the midfield after pressure in defence.

Defences Breaking Forward
(Fig 83)

The sight of a powerful and aggressive defender bringing the ball out and storming through the midfield can strike terror into the most confident opposition. This player must feel able to keep driving forward in the secure knowledge that a midfielder or attack will replace them behind and follow and support them if necessary.

Having brought the ball through the transition zone, the ball carrier may find, even after various midfield combinations, that there is no available cutter to use and the opposition are successfully steering her to the outside of the field. Having established that there are no open cutters in front of goal she should put the ball over the top and behind the goal causing the goalkeeper to turn and the defender's focus to change.

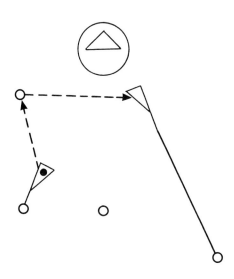

Fig 83 *Defence/midfielder, on the same team, cuts down the back-door channel as opposing defender's eyes check the ball.*

This is now the moment for the incoming cutter to receive the feed from behind and to shoot as the goalkeeper's head moves.

THE CRITICAL SHOOTING ZONE

As a team enters the critical shooting zone their first thought will be to threaten the goal and to drive forcefully forward looking for the shot. Attacks will be hoping for only one defender ahead to beat. For the most part, in the game today they will be confronted by two or three; if they manage to isolate one defender they should consider themselves very fortunate and take them on immediately. They may fake to go one side of the defender and then drive with acceleration the opposite way. They may stutter-step straight at the defence's body and as she begins to lean, break to the other side. Attacks in this area should always be looking to shoot or combine with a team-mate to exploit available space and create a scoring opportunity.

There are a multitude of creative moves, having arrived in the critical shooting zone, which should be attempted as initial drives on goal before the attack needs to employ other tactics. The ball may have been sent behind from the transition move and the receiver may see her opportunity to drive round the crease and shoot before too many defenders get back. Also, if the ball has been sent forward on the wing, a midfielder or defence may seize the opportunity to cut for goal on the blind side of defenders, down the back-door channel. Once the attack realise that their initial attempts at scoring plays have not been successful, and the opposition have managed to move back and surround the 'hole', then the moment has come to work together as a unit to create other chances.

Team Attack

Settled Attack

Perimeter   *(Fig 84)*

Having recognised the moment to settle, all attacking players up near the goal must re-organise their positioning and form a balanced, calm and disciplined ring around the goal using the 15m line as a general guide. Having established their perimeter as a unit the attacks must ensure safe team possession whilst employing the following principles:

(a)   There needs to be movement in the perimeter to force defenders to readjust and make decisions. This may be moving the ball around from one player to the next or the ball carrier running the ball round to another position.

(b)   As the next available receiver round the ring, an attack should move towards the ball carrier with her stick open to the outside of the perimeter.

(c)   All passing round must be flat, direct and on the outside of the ring.

(d)   Players must be constantly alert to fill gaps and keep the perimeter balanced.

(e)   All receivers must threaten the goal and make defenders think that they are a constant danger and about to drive. As they threaten, they should be checking the 'hole' for an open cutter.

(f)   All attacking players in a settled attack should be seeking to occupy the attention of their opponent at all times. This makes it more difficult for that defence to help out a team-mate in her defending unit.

Cut and Fill   *(Figs 85 & 86)*

Having established their disciplined peri-meter the attacks are now in a position to cut in towards the goal. The player opposite the ball on the circle cuts across to receive and shoot. The other attacks move and adjust their positions to fill the gaps and to back up the shot and the pass should they go astray. *(Fig 86)*.

Cutters should be aware of when they are at the opposite end of an optimum cutting channel (*see* Chapter 1 on shooting, page 14) to the ball and can cut towards it. If a player cuts for the feed and is not used she should move out and join the perimeter ahead as other players move to fill the gaps.

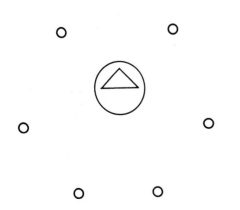

Fig 84   *Perimeter attack.*

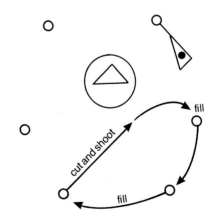

Fig 85   *'Cut and fill'.*

Fig 86   *An attack waits behind goal either as a support or to field a loose ball if the shot misses.*

Give and Go   *(Fig 87)*

By establishing eye contact with the next team-mate round the ring, using quick footwork and sharp, accurate passing the combination play of 'give and go' can be used from the perimeter most effectively. O^1 having given the ball to O^2 cuts immediately to the inside of her defence, asking for the ball by her ear. The stick is protected from the defender, is not extended away from the body, and is in a good position to fire a shot quickly.

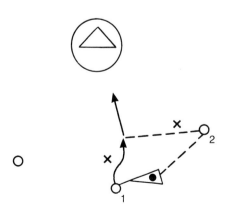

Fig 87   *'Give and go'.*

Draw and Dump (Scissors)   *(Fig 88)*

In this basic move of settled attack a player on the perimeter combines with an adjacent team-mate to deliberately deceive a defender and cause her to move. This creates 'a hole in the defender's bucket' into which the ball carrier can drive forward. Initially, the ball carrier must communicate by eye contact or signal with the player who is on her stick side. This player cuts across in front, calling very loudly for the ball. Her defender will be attracted by the call and will mark the cutter thinking she may be about to receive. This creates a gap in the defence into which the ball carrier can drive forward and either

75

Team Attack

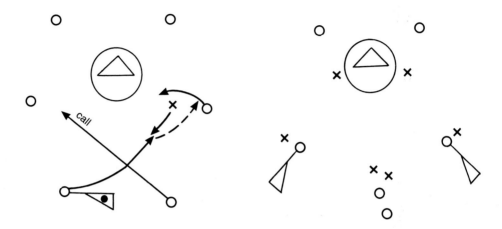

Fig 88   'Draw and dump'.

Fig 89   Stacking.

shoot or 'dump' the ball to another player near the crease, having drawn their defence. This is a very precise form of the scissors move where timing and accuracy are vital. All other players must be totally aware and understand what is happening so that they do not cut and confuse the move in progress.

Stacking   (Fig 89)

Instead of changing places with an adjacent attack the two players may move into a stacking formation at the front of the perimeter and confuse their defenders by drawing them close together. A variety of combinations are possible from this arrangement but all players in the perimeter need to work to ensure that the stacking pair are given time and space to work a move in this confined area. Having recognised the stack formation, the players on either side of it should move outwards round the ring to

clear their defender from the pair making the play. Alternatively, they can immediately face mark their defender and position to prevent their movement into the 'hole' to help out. Equally, the two attacks behind goal should be working to occupy the attention of their defences on the posts.

Pick Opposite   (Figs 90 & 91)

In pick opposite, the ball carrier will pass the ball one way on the perimeter and immediately move the opposite way to set a pick for an incoming cutter. Timing is vital as there may be only a split second gained before defences readjust. The player setting the pick must be within the visual field of defenders and the cutter must ensure that she passes the pick very closely and moves off the pick, accelerating and signalling clearly with eye contact and an open stick.

In Fig 90, O^1 passes the ball behind the goal then moves the opposite way to set a pick for O^2 who drives round, receives the feed and shoots.

Pick opposite is a move involving a screen for the cutter to receive the feed. There are moments in settled attack where teammates set a pick for the ball carrier to give her more time and space. This more frequently occurs near the crease where a pick prevents the defence following her opponent as she drives round the circle for a shot.

Outside the Perimeter   *(Figs 92 & 93)*

Midfield players not directly involved in the perimeter play should be constantly aware of, supporting and backing up the play in progress. Sometimes a fast move by a defender breaking forward into the settle, often on the blind side of defences, can be very effective. *(Fig 92).*

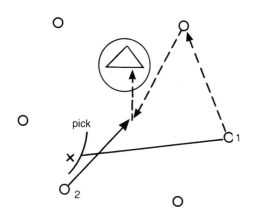

Fig 90   Pick opposite using behind the goal player – O¹ setting a pick for O².

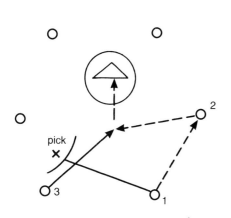

Fig 91   Pick opposite – setting a pick using three players in front of goal.

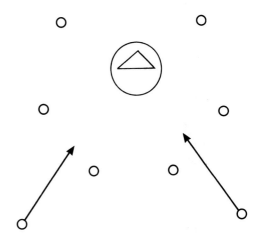

Fig 92   Midfield defender breaking through into the settle to attack.

77

Team Attack

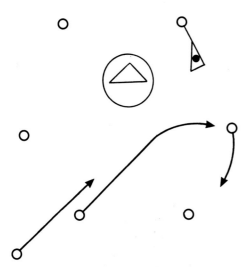

Fig 93 Midfield player acting as a second cutter.

Set plays can only arise from a disciplined calm. When the play signal has been called everyone in the perimeter must abandon thoughts of any other move and concentrate on the part they have to play in the forthcoming plan. Let us look at the movement involved in an *overload* set play. This is one of the simplest set plays, where one side of the goal is overloaded with players, leaving the other side available for a good dodging ball carrier to drive into.

The signal comes initially from the attack leader, or from a player in a feeding position behind the goal. She passes to an adjacent team-mate who then changes places with her and becomes the dodging ball carrier. This player drives round the back of the goal and comes forward into an empty space for the shot. Players who *were* on this side have rushed across the 'hole' asking for the ball

They may also become a second cutter because space has opened up when the first cutter on a line was not used. (*Fig 93*).

Set Plays *(Fig 94)*

A set play is a series of well-organised moves usually involving all members of the perimeter. It is vitally important that all players taking part understand the sequence and timing and know the role they each will have in order that the set play successfully ends in a goal. All the strategies mentioned up to now in settled attack can occur spontaneously. They involve two or three players and require cue reading and good awareness. A set play requires considerable practice and repetition to achieve the perfect timing and sharpness necessary for success and is often a larger strategy involving a combination of smaller moves.

The possibilities are endless for the inventive coach with plenty of team practice time for repetition.

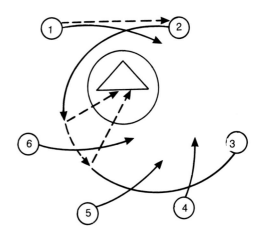

Fig 94 Overload set play.

and drawing their defences across with
them. The player who was next to the new
receiver cuts round the front in the opposite
direction and makes herself available, backing up the driving ball carrier in case she
needs to pass if her shot is denied.

1.   Feeder 1 passes to 2, cuts inside her
and picks her defender. (*Fig 94*).
2.   Ball carrier 2 drives round the crease
looking for the angle to shoot.
3.   As the pass goes, 4, 5 and 6 cut across
towards the receiver, calling loudly and
signalling as cutters.
4.   As these players cut, player 3, who is
already on that side, cuts the opposite way
to meet the ball carrier as she comes round.
She becomes an alternative for the driver,
who can now shoot or pass to this backing-
up player if she meets problems.

This set play can of course be reversed to
drive round the opposite side of the goal.
Teams will develop their own timings, cues
and adjustments the more the set play is
rehearsed. Some teams choose to have the
same players in specific positions each
time, whereas others prefer that all players
understand and can fulfil the demands of
each role.

Settled Attack with Crease Player   (Figs 95 & 96)

This is a development from a pure perimeter
and opens up other possibilities in play.
   Playing with a crease player has to be
used with a clear understanding of its possibilities within the game today. (*Fig 95*). The
rules relating to the space in front of goal
and the number of players generally involved in the area will greatly influence the
use of this player. A crease player needs to
be an excellent shooter, capable of safe

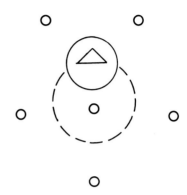

Fig 95   Settled attack with crease player.

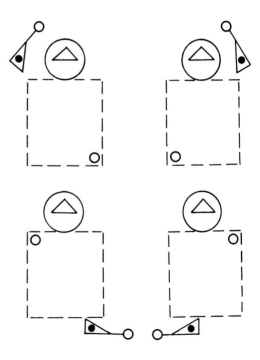

Fig 96   Positioning of the crease player
relative to the feeder.

handling under extreme pressure. She often has little more than one step to make space and present her target. She has to be able to convert hard feeds instantaneously.

The crease-position player works very hard, too, for the benefit of others in the perimeter, constantly changing her position to set picks for incoming cutters. She relates continuously to where the ball is – moving opposite to the ball position in an oblong area in front of the goal crease, e.g. when the ball is behind, she will move out from the circle diagonally opposite the ball, and when the ball is at the front of the perimeter she will move back nearer the crease. (*Fig 96*).

The crease player is positioned so that incoming cutters using her as a pick have adequate space behind them to receive the feed and shoot.

The crease attack can also be responsible for screening the goalie's vision for incoming shots. Longer shots from just outside the perimeter can be very difficult for a goalkeeper if her line of vision is screened and she cannot follow the flight of the ball. The screening attack should line up with the goalkeeper and a point well over on the ball carrier's stick side. She should not line up with the body as it is the stick head that must be screened. She waits for the shot to pass by, moving to the side at the last moment, or jumping over a low shot and then turning, looking for the rebound off the goalie's stick or body.

Breaking a Defence Zone   *(Figs 97–100)*

A team cannot play its normal attacking moves if the opposition has chosen to play zone defence. Such a system requires defenders to cover specific areas of the field and any attacker who happens to be in that area. This is a different philosophy to a normal system which is man-to-man based and means each defender must relate to an individual attack regardless of where they go. The 'bucket' defence system is based on man-to-man play where individuals relate together to create strength as a unit.

In attacking a zone, the defenders must be forced into adjusting to the ball as it is passed round the perimeter. Shots will only be possible though if there is movement of players as well as the ball. Attacking a zone requires considerable patience and careful, accurate passing. The ball needs to move very quickly, but safe team possession is of paramount importance. The feeders at the back of the goal must look for opportunities to feed the ball to open cutters who are in a position to shoot. If no one is open for the shot they must keep the ball moving between themselves and other adjacent players in the perimeter. Attacks must work constantly to make the zone react and adjust. If individuals are continuously moved, then gaps and spaces will open up for a shot. Individuals in the zone must be made to cope with opponents as well as ball position. This can be done by placing attacks inside the zone and by cutters constantly penetrating the zone area.

There are basic pointers to remember when attempting to break a zone:

1.   Keep putting the ball behind goal so that goalkeeper and defences are made to turn their heads.
2.   Unproductive cuts are a waste of time and energy. All cuts should cut through the zone and to the ball.
3.   Attacks should place themselves on and out along the 'seams' of a zone. (*Fig 97*). This way defences wonder who should be responsible for the cutter. Other attacks must keep moving to keep the vision of

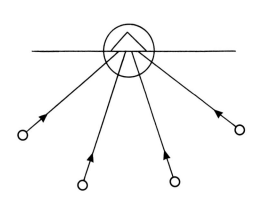

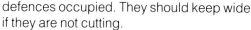

Fig 97   Attacks should place themselves on the 'seams' of the zone.

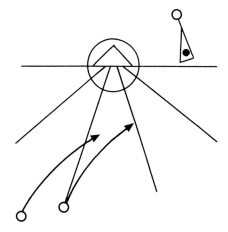

Fig 98   Second cutter into the zone.

defences occupied. They should keep wide if they are not cutting.

4.   Aim to make the zone collapse positionally by drawing the defence to one area and passing the ball quickly to another. This can be done by concentrating the passing on one back corner of the zone. If adjacent players in this area pass the ball between themselves many times, the players in the zone have to readjust on each ball position. As this is repeated, they become mesmerised and gradually get drawn out of position by constant readjustment. When this happens the ball must be swung across quickly and fed to a cutter using the enlarged space.

5.   In a man-to-man bucket system, defenders will escort a cutter from one side of the perimeter, through the 'hole', until they join the perimeter on the opposite side. In zone defence, a player stays with the cutter as she enters her area and then passes her on to the team-mate guarding the next sector of

the zone. It is possible to exploit this fact by using a second cutter immediately after the first, using the same line and the same sector of the zone. (*Fig 98*). It is better to use a player driving forward from the midfield as the second cutter, whilst others in the perimeter keep moving to occupy the attention of defences near them.

6.   At least one attacking player should endeavour to be in the zone, in the 'hole' area. A player in the middle always causes worry as the defence there has to cope with her all the time. She can create confusion by simply interchanging position with others on the perimeter as the ball is moved. This may be by passing or by the feeder running to the point of the goal behind, turning and running back to the feeding position.

As in perimeter play, a crease player must work opposite to the ball in an oblong space in front of goal. She must be a constant nuisance to the defence, working to get her stick open, and looking as though she is

Team Attack

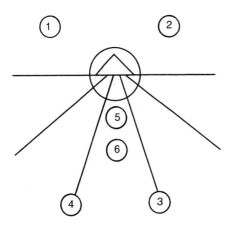

Fig 99   Two players inside the zone.

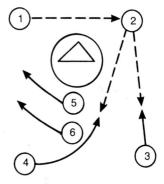

Fig 100   Set play based on the overload principle.

about to receive the feed at any moment. The low reception of a feed at about knee level can be very effective as zone players tend to 'think high' and have their sticks raised up.

It is also possible to have two players inside the zone, one near the crease and one further forward. (*Fig 99*).

These two players are constantly working to get open, changing places or setting picks for each other. If they really look dangerous the zone starts paying attention and spaces appear for perimeter players to cut in and shoot.

It is possible with these two players inside the zone to organise a set play based on the

overload principle. This is similar to the set play from the perimeter but spatially different because of the zone. (*Fig 100*).

The ball is with feeder 1 behind the goal. The two inside players 5 and 6 cut towards the ball.

The feeder fakes the pass but actually passes to the second feeder behind goal. This feeder passes to another cutter (3 or 4) coming in from the front of the perimeter.

There are many set plays possible for an attack group involving a combination of different moves which demand considerable player movement and patience to wait for the cutter to be really open and available.

6 Team Defence

Team defence involves *twelve* people, not just those players who are named as defences, and starts as soon as the opposition gain possession.

It is very important that every player can defend and knows what to do in various situations on the field. If, for example, third man goes into attack with the ball, third home must not only be capable of individual defence play but must be able to slot into the defence unit should third man remain in attack for the rest of that move. The days of an attack player waving her stick at her defence, chasing for a few token steps, then watching her disappear for 'the defence' to take care of, are gone.

Every team member should be aware of the sequence of defence play from the moment the opposing goalkeeper initiates the attack to the moment a shot is taken. Remember there are three main areas to defend:

● The *clearing zone* – where the opponents attempt to move the ball from their goal to the midfield.
● The *transition zone* – where the opponents attempt to move the ball through the centre to connect with their attack players.
● The *critical shooting zone* – where the opponents aim is to feed or take the ball into a scoring position.

THE CLEARING ZONE

Denial Defence

Once the opposing goalkeeper has the ball it is vital that the homes and attack wings think about defence immediately. Too often there is a feeling of dismay and a 'slump' when a shot is saved and possession lost. This is the moment the opposition can use to advantage to start clearing the ball upfield.

The defending homes and wings can make a big difference if they look up and around right away, move to pick up the nearest player and put pressure on the clear. The goalkeeper has ten seconds to make the clear safely and will feel anxiety if all her defence unit are closely marked. There must be a concerted effort by all the attack players, otherwise a passing option will quickly open up. Denial defence and the use of the extended stick are useful defensive ploys here, particularly as the clears are usually aimed at the outside of the field for safety. An attack who covers the passing lane forces her defence to come back upfield for a short clear, and can then pressure the ball, steering, slowing, and, if possible, tackling to regain possession. A player, whose defence has stayed back to cover the clear, may be able to help her team-mate, whose opponent has the ball, by chasing upfield and double teaming. This again puts pressure on the clearing defence, perhaps forcing a rushed pass which can be intercepted.

Certainly if an opponent gets ahead and runs up the field with the ball, she must be chased right through to the moment the ball is released. There is a chance then that any team-mate taking the player on upfield would slow her down sufficiently for a double team to take place. No self-respecting attack unit allows opponents to clear the ball out of their area without being chased and hassled. Only with this kind of determined pressure can the defence unit at the other end of the field do their job effectively.

Zone Press   *(Fig 101)*

The above ideas for defending the clearing zone are based on fundamental man-to-man technique, i.e. denial defence, covering the passing lanes, steering, tackling and double teaming. However, an attack unit can work together in a form of zone called a *zone press* which uses double teaming and zoning together. Zoning is a form of defence which involves covering a space rather than a player. A zone press uses the players furthest away from the ball as a zone whilst the players nearest the ball pressure the ball carrier.

The first move allows the goalkeeper to make a short clear since the attack unit moves immediately to form a zone furthest up the field. Once the clear is made, the nearest two players pressure the ball carrier with the next two players denying the nearest and safest passes. The players furthest from the ball zone cover the remaining space.

This is not a simple plan to execute because of the space involved. The larger the space the more difficult it is to make a zone work. However, the element of surprise can often cause the defence player, who is suddenly double teamed, to panic and thus lose possession. Once the players with the

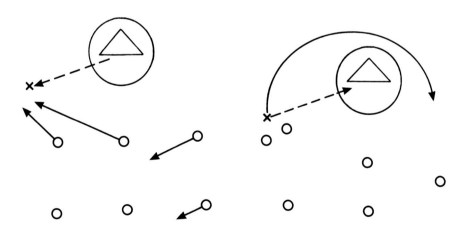

Fig 101   Zone press which forces either a back pass or a move behind the goal.

ball realise a zone is being used they can clear back to the goalkeeper, or run round the back of the goal and clear to the free side which is being covered by the zoning players. (*Fig 101*). However, recognition of a tactic is often slow and, if various ideas are used, the opponents could be fooled. Whatever the plan used to defend the clear, it must be understood by all the attack unit and must be a totally determined and full-blooded effort. Good defence at this point, before the clearing pattern gets underway, could mean an immediate second chance for a shot. That is worth working for.

THE TRANSITION ZONE

As the ball moves into the midfield the attacking team will be attempting to make connecting moves upfield so that the ball can come out of the clearing zone and into the shooting area. Remember the general aim will be to bring the ball into the centre of the field and direct it towards the goal area. Therefore any player whose opponent is bringing the ball into the midfield should attempt to steer them to the outside of the field and to slow them down. Passing options are immediately decreased. (*Fig 102*).

Passing Options *(Figs 103–106)*

When a player is steered to the edge of the field, all other attacks who have been marking in the clearing zone should stay with their opponents so that they are prevented from giving support to the ball carrier in the midfield.

Defences already in the midfield, or in the shooting zone, should be alert now and ready to cut off passing options. The attacking

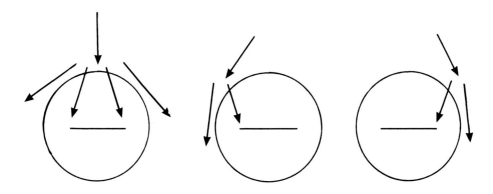

Fig 102   Passing options in the midfield.

85

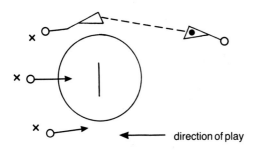

Fig 103 *Connecting cuts allowed*

← direction of play

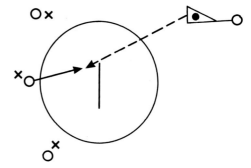

Fig 105 *Transition zone is crossed.*

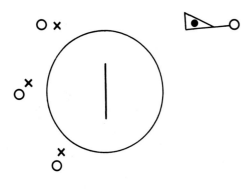

Fig 104 *Connecting cuts denied.*

team will want to make connecting cuts towards the player coming out with the ball. (*Fig 103*). If the transition zone is not to be conceded, then all defences should be denying the cut and covering the passing lane. (*Fig 104*). This type of defence must be agreed by all the defence unit. Only then can it be effective, since one attack left open will mean the ball can be passed and the transition made. (*Fig 105*).

Denial defence is a very challenging and rewarding form of defence, and requires determination and fitness from all the defence unit. It forces errors and means that every defence has a chance to be first onto a loose ball because of their positioning. (*Fig 106*). However, not all defence units may be ready to cope with this exciting and attacking form of defending the transition zone. A less fit, slow, or newly formed defence unit may have to concede the mid-field connection, though they can still mark tightly, just goal-side of their opponents,

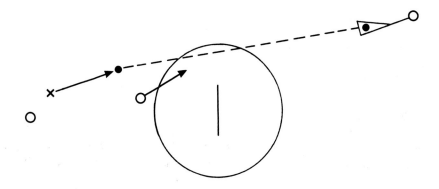

Fig 106   Loose ball is snapped up by the next defence.

ready to check, intercept or go for a loose ball. Positioning for this method of defence must take into account the pathway the attacks want to move on, having received the connecting pass. Remember an attack wants to go straight to goal, so the defence unit should place itself so that moves are always made to the outside of the field.

The Fast Break

In the women's game, where players can move into either half of the field and numbers and space are unrestricted, unlike the men's game, the midfield area is extremely important. It can mean the difference between a winning or a losing team. An attack gains momentum through the midfield. Fast breaks start here as a player moves through unmarked. Fluency and rhythm can grow, or be broken up, by what happens on transition. A team that struggles to get the ball through this zone has to set up an attack

later on when the defence are nicely settled and in position.

If a fast break does occur, it will be necessary for the defence to 'slide', that is the defence ahead of the free player with the ball moves off her own player onto the free player to force her to pass or dodge or slow down. As the defence slides, the next defence nearest the new free player starts to adjust. All defences can make the fast break more difficult by: (a) the timing of their move, (b) the adjustment of position to cover space, (c) the use of a high stick to block the ball or cover space.

The defence needs to judge her movement so that the attack is not sure whether to run or pass. A hovering defence, who relates both to her own attack and the free player by extending her stick and choosing a pathway that covers the potential passing lane, can make a free attack doubt her decision. That is the first chink in the armour.

If the fast break happens closer to the

goal, towards the end of the transition zone, a defence unit may decide to run back, cut their losses and form a defensive zone. This is covered later in this chapter.

Attacks may not have created an overlap, or fast-break situation, but may work together to confuse the defence by swinging the ball or working in small units in a 'give and go', scissors or stacking manoeuvre. Swinging the ball makes the defence have to adjust their positioning very quickly over large spaces. It is vital that defences on the far side of the transition zone are alert and ready to intercept any ball that is suddenly swung across the field. Even though they are so far away from the ball carrier, the defence must be aware of what is happening on the ball.

Communication

In the unit manoeuvres, such as scissors or stacking, the attack aim to confuse the defence by running into the same small space. A pick uses the same idea. Here it is vital that defences learn to recognise what is happening. They will have to decide quickly whether they are able to stay with their own attack. An alert defence will call, 'Switch', and initiate a change of focus if she can see her pathway to her attack being cut off. Even more important is the ability to recognise a pick. Again, the knowledgeable defence will give early warning and the defence unit can try to adjust. All defences must be able to recognise such instances and communicate with each other.

THE CRITICAL SHOOTING ZONE

Man-to-Man Defence

Inevitably, however good a defence unit is, the ball will get through the midfield into the area in which a goal-scoring opportunity exists. This is the point at which the defences have to divide their attention much more evenly between their opponent, the ball carrier, and the critical shooting area in front of the goal.

At this point, when the ball has reached the opposition's half of the field, no defence should be behind the ball, i.e. further away from goal than the ball carrier as they cannot be of assistance from this position.

Helping Defence

As a connecting pass is made, or as a player carries the ball out of the transition zone, all defences should adjust their position to keep ahead of the ball.

X^2 is well ahead of the ball and has also moved in towards the goal into a covering position. This is a 'helping' defence unit. (*Fig 107*).

Bucket Defence   (Figs 108–114)

It is these two adjustments, that is, keeping ahead of the ball and moving in to cover from the side furthest away from the ball, that bring about the so-called 'bucket' defence used to defend the shooting area. (*Fig 108*). The defences circle the space from which a shot can be taken once their attempts to gain possession further upfield have failed. Although they are still responsible for their own opponent, they are also aware of each other, and of the space they

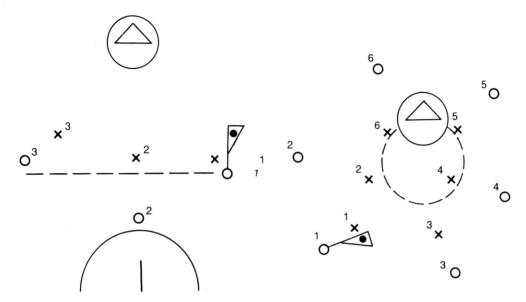

Fig 107   *All defences keep ahead of the ball.*

Fig 109   *The 'bucket' adjusts according to the position of the ball.*

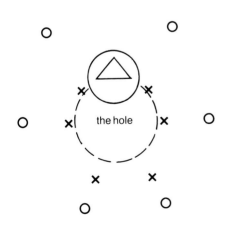

Fig 108   *The 'bucket'.*

are protecting. Any defence moving away from the bucket shape leaves a vulnerable area for the attack to penetrate. Notice how the shape and positioning of the defence unit adjusts in relation to the position of the ball. X^4 and X^5 have dropped in towards the goal on the far side to cover and pick up any dangerous centre or right-wing breaks. X^3 is in a good position to slide and cover for X^1 should O^1 drive to the right. (*Figs 109 & 110*).

If any attack cuts through the space to goal, her defence follows her and tries to put herself ball-side of the cutter to prevent a feed for the shot. She then repositions on the edge of the 'bucket' opposite to where her attack positions and adjusts to the ball position. (*Fig 111*).

If an attack goes into the 'hole', the critical scoring area, and stays there, then the defence must stay with her. If the ball is in front of goal the best position is denial. (*Figs 112 & 113*). If the ball is behind goal, then face

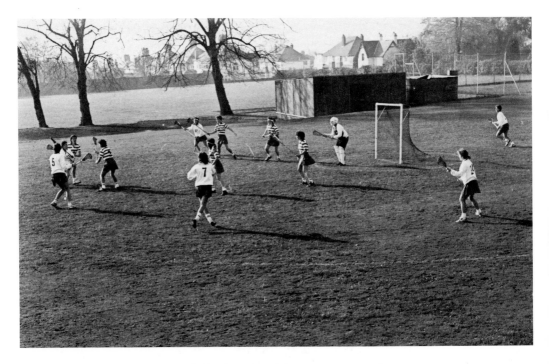

Figs 110(a) & (b)   'Bucket' defence. Defenders cover their own opponent and
also adjust towards the ball carrier and towards the 'hole'.

Fig 110(b)

marking may be best with the goalkeeper giving information about ball position. This attack player is extremely dangerous since a feed to her stick can be 'quick-sticked' straight into the goal. The defence's stick should cover her stick head at all times.

There are many individual ideas that defences can develop with experience to cover cutters and static attacks, but the main criterion must be to be in the best position to see the ball, the player and the 'hole'. Only in the instance mentioned above would face marking be even a possibility (because the attack is obviously in a key shooting position). Otherwise a defence who is caught 'player watching' or 'ball watching' at this point can be the weakness in the team that the attack penetrates.

When the ball is behind goal all the defence have a sighting problem, particularly the goalkeeper, and communication

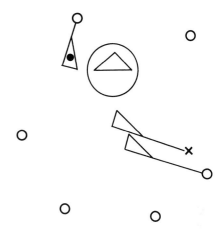

Fig 111 Defence covering the passing lane of the feeder to the cutter.

Fig 112(a) A cutter makes a goal cut which is denied by the defender.

Fig 112(b) The feeder swings the ball out to the wing as she sees the goal cut denied.

Team Defence

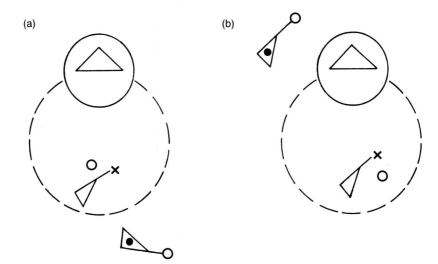

(a)   (b)

Fig 113   Marking a player in the 'hole'.

and cover are vital. Whilst in the 'bucket' the defence unit must talk to each other in a calm and confident way. Every defence has a job to do and it is excellent training to have to say what that job is at each point of play as briefly as possible, such as:

– 'Got the ball', i.e. I am covering the player with the ball.
– 'Got you right', i.e. I am ready to double team or slide on your right.
– 'Got the back door', i.e. I am covering the cut from the side furthest from the ball.
– 'Ready to slide', i.e. I am ready to take on your opponent if you go to help elsewhere.

Sometimes it is easier to change opponents rather than move with them. For example, in a scissors movement with O^1 and O^2 it may be better for X^1 to pick up O^2 and vice versa. (*Fig 114*). Defences should call, 'Switch', to avoid confusion.

It is easy to see why defences prefer

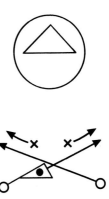

Fig 114   Defence switch opponents.

'practising' in games – so many of their skills are team-unit skills, based on mutual understanding and constant repetition of movements.

Sliding   *(Figs 115–118)*

When players are confident in each other they can develop moves that put extra pressure on the attack. For example, a basic defence unit may initially leave the attack behind goal free since she is less dangerous than those in front, even when she has the ball. However, it can be very effective to pressure a good feeder behind goal. Everyone must know what is happening and adjust the slide accordingly. (*Fig 115*). Attack wings can help here by being ready to move into defence to help cover. Another situation could arise where the defence

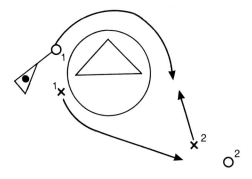

Fig 116   Defences switching roles and opponents.

switch roles because the attack with the ball crosses behind the goal and X^1 for some reason cannot get round. X^2 moves in to cover. X^1 takes O^2. (*Fig 116*). Again the defence must call, 'Switch'. Sometimes two attacks go behind the goal and pass the ball from side to side, looking for a cutter. Again pressure can be put on by both defences, as long as they work together, and defences in front realise what is happening. Attack wings often find themselves helping out in 'the bucket' and can be very useful extra players if pressure is being put on behind goal. (*Fig 117*).

All defences should be sure to use the full extension of their stick to cover the space above and within the 'hole'. A defence unit looks much bigger if sticks are extended.

Defence of the shooting area has so far been based on equal numbers. However, there will always be the fast break when attacks create an overlap and have one, or even two, extra players. At this point the

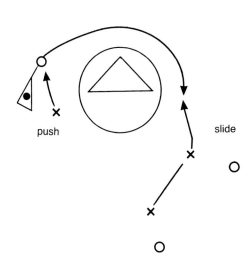

Fig 115   Defences 'pushing' and 'sliding'.

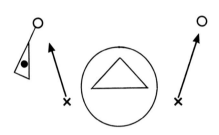

Fig 117   Simultaneous pressure put on both
attacks behind goal.

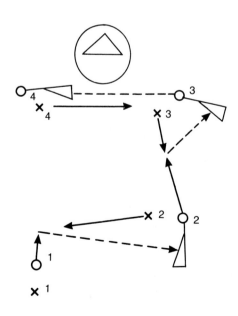

Fig 118   Sliding to cope with a free attack.

defence cannot play one-on-one or double team. As a unit they need to slow down the break, force passes and cover space, while the defence unit reassembles and reorganises.

The simplest way to cover is to slide from a player without the ball onto the ball carrier. However, eventually, unless the attack makes a mistake, or the defence left behind catches up, there will be an attack free to take the shot. (*Fig 118*).

Emergency Triangle   *(Fig 119)*

In a 4 v 3 situation it may be wiser for the defence to consolidate their defensive position to cover the shooting area and form a small zone. This is sometimes called the emergency triangle.

The triangle is formed by the three defences, on a set signal, perhaps given by the goalkeeper. They chase back to goal at full speed, calling their positions as 'Back left', 'Back right' and 'Point'. Point is the player at the point of the triangle who takes on the ball carrier (not the position point). Each player repositions according to the ball movement. (*Fig 119*).

Any 4 v 3 situation should result in a goal. The emergency triangle is a stop-gap measure and immediately the fourth defence gets back, the defence unit works man-to-man again. This also requires the defence to communicate with each other. In all defence play near goal, good positioning and the use of a high, extended stick can make the space available seem much less than it really is. Defences should be constantly urged to think where their own opponent wants to move, and also where the danger points are in relation to the ball carrier and other players. Experience brings better anticipation of what could happen, and defences learn from talking through situations together.

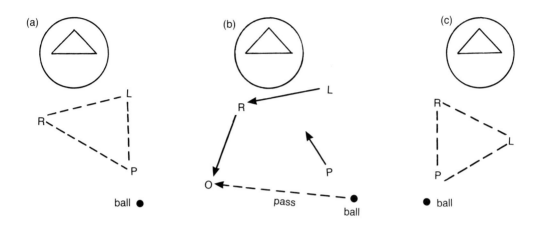

Fig 119(a)   Emergency triangle.

Fig 119(b)   Repositioning to cover the new ball carrier.

Fig 119(c)   New triangle.

Working in practice with an umpire, or with an extra pair of eyes behind the ball carrier, will help the defence unit become aware of the shooting space, i.e. the space between the potential shooter and the goal, which must not be blocked by a defence unless an attack is also in that space. All work as a defence unit must be developed with an awareness of keeping the shooting space unblocked.

Zone Defence

The concept of a zone involves defending territory rather than players. It is both useful and practical in some contexts, but whilst there is a rule that forbids defences from standing in the shooting area, zoning can be difficult to execute, except by a tactically aware defence unit.

We strongly suggest teaching man-to-man defence first since zoning requires many of the basic skills already mentioned.

It is the defence unit's focus and positioning that is different.

A zone could be used for a variety of reasons:

● It forces attacks to take the shot from outside the zone, which could be useful if your defenders are strong but the goal-keeper weak or inexperienced.
● The opposition might depend on attacks who like to dodge and take on isolated defences. They would find a zone difficult to cope with.
● It may be necessary to change the flow or momentum of the opposition's play.
● The defence may be having trouble dealing with the speed and passing skills of the attack.

A zone is not static if it is working well. It is constantly moving and putting pressure on opponents in the critical shooting zone. It adapts to the position of the ball and is completely dependent upon good communication between players. A tactically sound goalkeeper is a great asset in making a zone successful. The principles to consider when setting up a zone are simple, but the execution requires constant practice. Zoning could be used as the major defensive tactic, but it is also possible to use it as an alternative development from man-to-man systems.

Principles of Zone Defence *(Fig 120)*

1. The danger area around the goal is basically divided into segments for which each defender is responsible. (*Fig 120*).
2. The defender adjusts her position in the segment according to: (a) the position of the ball, (b) any opponent who enters her segment.

3. A zone always sets up from near the goal outwards so that there is always back-up.
4. Pressure must always be placed on the ball carrier entering the segment.
5. Since a zone defence is positioned to cover spaces, defenders should be positioned according to their strengths and the zone's weakness. Moves tend to be made round the goal crease where back-up is difficult and defences can leave gaps if they are inexperienced at working round the crease.
6. Defenders should use the triangle principle mentioned in man-to-man defence, constantly relating to any player in their part of the zone, the ball and the goal. Heads should be 'on swivels'.
7. Sticks should be held up and towards the inside of the zone.
8. Positioning should be such that the pass to the cutter is covered as she moves across your segment. The cutter is followed then 'handed over' to the defender in the next segment of the zone.
9. Talk is essential if players are to be covered by the zone defence. Warnings need to be given about cutters, ball position, tackles and sliding.

Setting up a Zone *(Figs 121 & 122)*

As the zone is being set up, the ball carrier must be pressured and slowed down. We have already discussed about the emergency triangle where, within the man-to-man defence system, defences as a last resort might use a mini zone of three defences to cope with a fast breaking attack unit with extra players. If a team is setting up a zone, then the triangle forms the basic shape on which the zone builds. (*Fig 121*).

It is important that the back players retreat as fast as possible to defend the space in

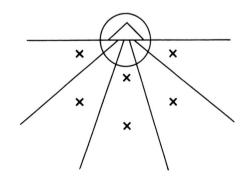

Fig 120   Positioning of a zone.

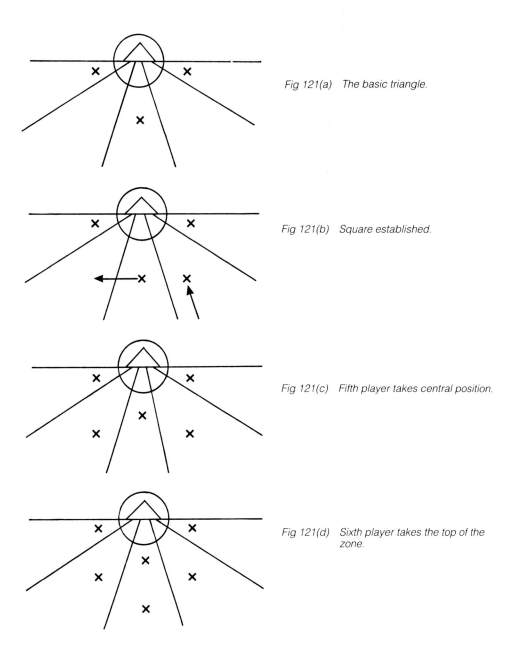

Fig 121(a)   The basic triangle.

Fig 121(b)   Square established.

Fig 121(c)   Fifth player takes central position.

Fig 121(d)   Sixth player takes the top of the zone.

Fig 121   Building a zone.

Team Defence

front of goal. They then turn out to face the ball, sticks high and to the inside of the space. These players would usually include the defenders who are excellent at coping with moves around the crease and are good at reading the game.

The fourth player will complete the square and usually moves into the side away from the ball as the top of the triangle adjusts across to the ball.

The fifth player moves into the centre spot near the goal. This player must be aware of the shooting space when the ball is in front of the goal.

The sixth player sets up in the middle at the top of the zone furthest away from the goal.

The zone always positions according to where the ball is, just as in the helping man-to-man defence. The defence furthest away

from the ball comes in, leaving the furthest attack free and allowing pressure to be placed on the ball carrier.

If the ball goes behind goal it is possible to release players to chase and harass the ball carrier either from the zone or from the attack players up field. This requires excellent communication since a zone should always adjust its positioning from the back, the point furthest away from the ball, so that gaps do not appear within it. It is important that it is always the attack furthest away from the ball who is left open since it takes more time to get the ball to her and the zone has time to adjust. In the example shown in *Fig 122*, the defence have moved to cover the ball as it moves round the edge of the zone and have left a gap for the third attack to penetrate. It is better at this point for the middle defence to move forward and the

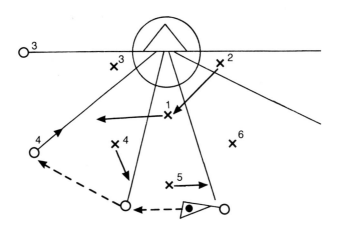

Fig 122   As defenders are drawn out of position a gap appears for O^4. X^1 moves forward, backed up by X^2, so that X^3 can cover the move by O^3 rather than leaving a gap near the crease.

back defence to move to the middle, rather than use the outer defender near the crease. Her move across would leave a big gap for the fourth attacker to penetrate unopposed.

Any cutter who comes through the zone, or any attack who stands within the zone, must be marked since this is the shooting area. Defences must call 'Cutter' to alert the next defence to be ready to take on the cutter within their segment. Obviously the middle section of the cut is most dangerous since the best shot can be taken from there. As soon as the player has been escorted through the segment, the defender should immediately move back into a covering position, watching the ball and checking that a second cutter is not coming through. Attacks will usually cut from the blind side and this is why communication is absolutely vital for all the defence.

There are various patterns which a zone can use and the plan must take account of the rule structure in use and the space involved. Unlike most other games, lacrosse uses the space behind goal and consequently the edges of the crease are a weak point in the zone. Since the ball can be passed round in a complete circle, the adjustment of the defence unit is quite considerable, as is the area they need to cover visually. Plans may need to be adjusted, therefore, if it is known that one of the attacks always uses a feeder from behind the goal. The strategy might be consistently to pressure that feeder by pushing one of the zone behind goal and filling in with attack players in front of goal. The zone would then make cutting difficult whilst the feeder is being forced to adjust to a defence who is pressuring and distracting her.

As rules develop, it may become more or less difficult to play a zone. Space in front of goal at present is kept open by the rule on shooting space and a zone would need to be very aware of keeping the space between the ball carrier and the goal free of static defenders unless, of course, an attack was also in that space. Basketball and men's lacrosse are both sports that have used and developed the concepts of zone defence and could be used as a source of ideas to adapt and make relevant to the women's game.

7   Coaching

In this chapter are set out concepts and principles on which our coaching philosophy is based. It is not a practical coaching guide since this is available through the various Coaching Awards set out by the Women's and Men's Lacrosse Associations. We also include several sources of information on the psychology and physiology of team preparation.

It is important that the analysis of the game in preceding chapters is matched by an explanation of our beliefs about the coaching and teaching of a team game such as lacrosse.

COACHING CONCEPTS

1.   Players should know all the possibilities and alternatives open to them wherever they find themselves in the game.
2.   Players should be coached from the very beginning to be aware of the whole field of play and to make sound judgements based on what they see in the game.
3.   Players need to practise making decisions and choosing appropriate actions. Making decisions is a key element of any game. Technical skill is not enough.
4.   Players should be encouraged to assess the playing conditions of the day, judge the strengths and weaknesses of their opponents, and be able to adapt accordingly.
5.   Players should feel involved in, and committed to, the ideas and concepts being developed. They should feel encouraged to contribute their own ideas.
6.   Players are all different and need individual help to develop coping strategies in competition. The coach must recognise when, and in what way, players need support to function effectively under pressure.
7.   Effective communication channels need to be established so that players and coach feel able to express feelings, ideas or anxieties openly.

Fig 123   A player blocks the defender's pathway whilst the ball carrier dodges through.

8. Players should be encouraged to take responsibility for their own performance and training. They should learn to make their own decisions, supported by the coach and team-mates and develop a perception of their role in the group.

9. Help must be given in a positive, encouraging way if players are to develop to their full potential.

10. A relaxed, positive attitude needs to be created so that there is neither fear of losing nor over-anxiety about winning.

11. A value needs to be placed on the way in which a game is played and won. Good play and good conduct should be both encouraged and expected by the coach.

UNDERSTANDING THE GAME

If a coach wants to develop players who can make decisions, choose appropriate actions and make sound judgements in the game, she must help them by presenting situations in which such skills can be practised.

First of all, we need to look at the demands of the game and analyse its component parts. These parts can be structured into practices that are realistic and closely related to the game. They are problems that occur in the game and which are isolated in practice so that questions can be asked. The questions might, for example, be about where and when to pass or shoot; they might also be about how effectively to combine with other team-mates to solve the problem. As a result of these questions and the ensuing answers, various techniques will be required. These can then be practised, if necessary, to increase the players' stock of vocabulary and their effectiveness within the game.

We do not recommend practising techniques unrelated to the game, except as a brisk tuning up at the beginning of a session. Of course, some strong, accurate passing sequences in shuttles are an excellent way to get the feet working, the eyes focused and concentration established before moving into the practice itself. We believe that players should understand the relevance of a technique to the game and practise it within that context. Players are often more motivated to practise and improve their individual technique when they can clearly see the value of its use in the game.

It is often said that if only a player's stickwork were better, then her performance in the game would improve. This implies that the only thing required to play well in a game is good stickwork. There is no doubt that a certain technical expertise, matched with speedy running, can allow a player some initial success. However, if the development of stickwork is not matched step by step with learning about the interaction and changing relationships with team-mates and opponents, then a player will soon be outplayed by more tactically aware opposition. Even when a technique is isolated for improvement, it should be constantly varied to match the changing situations in a game. For example, a two-handed pick up is often practised repetitively with an emphasis on foot position, strong scooping action and body over the ball. Yet in the game, when opposition are with you, the opportunity to pick up in the accepted way rarely occurs. Players need to consider what to do in relation to an opponent. This may mean flicking the ball to a free side, or stopping it quickly, or even picking up with one hand on the stick. The important point is to practise the real skill as it occurs within a fast-moving game and not in isolation.

From the earliest stage players can be

Coaching

encouraged to find out and suggest their own answers to some of the problems encountered in the game. Remember the game can be as small as 1 v 1 or the full 12 v 12 form. In a 2 v 1 game, for example, which starts with the ball being rolled for two players to chase, tactical questions about how to gain possession, how to protect the stick and where the third player indicates for the catch are all as important as the pure technique of picking up. We believe that all practices should have the potential for decision making as well as the demand for skilful performance. The two go hand in hand right from the start.

The use of the smaller game situation is crucial at all levels to give all players the chance to practise over and over again answering the problem posed. Half games, games with uneven opposition, e.g. 4 v 3, can be used to set up a particular situation met in the game. Starting the ball behind goal, out on the wing, or from a goal-clear, means that players have to read the situation and react to it quickly, assessing what they need to do and how they need to adjust and co-operate together to be effective. Here team unit possibilities arise that can be practised in smaller groups, such as double teaming in defence, or give and go in attack. However experienced the group, they still need constant practice in small games where they can repeat moves and participate in both attack and defence positions. All players should experience all aspects of team play whatever their age or expertise. Too many players come through to top levels of the sport as 'a centre' or 'a cover point' and have no broad understanding of the game as a whole, or any knowledge of how to play other positions on the field. The game, as played today, is very fluid, with free movement from end to end, and players must be adaptable and able to assume any role demanded of them.

Whilst practising, players should constantly be urged to assess their own opponent, and other players around them. Are they one-sided? Have they a particular weakness, such as poor handling of the ball under pressure? Are they slow off the mark? What are their strengths? Every player should watch the goalkeeper. How does she position? Does she prefer high shots to the low bounce?

Players should also assess their own team-mates and know what they can and cannot do. This requires great sensitivity and awareness, both of the players' abilities and of the general weather conditions. If there is a strong wind, or the sun is low, then movement for the ball needs to adjust accordingly. Many players blame conditions for their mistakes, yet the mistake is in not adjusting to the conditions.

Whilst it is the coach who usually initiates ideas, the players should be encouraged to evaluate those ideas and develop their own answers based on the principles behind the practice. Coaches can sometimes feel threatened by players who ask questions. Yet this is the first commitment by that player to the ideas being practised. Players should feel able to offer suggestions based on their own experience, and work on an idea in practices so that what develops is jointly owned by coach and players. It is a pity if coaches reject such experience since there is no substitute for playing the game. All such ideas need to be offered and received in a positive way so that neither coach nor player need feel undermined or unacknowledged. Coaches should not feel that they are the ultimate, and only, resource. They are a focus for ideas and overall planning, but within that structure there is room for contributions from many other sources.

MENTAL SKILLS

Attitudes

Understanding the game and its component parts is only part of the answer to successful competition. The development of a strong mental attitude is vital if a player is to produce her best performance under the pressures of competitive play.

Creating positive attitudes is one of the most important tasks for the coach. Criticism need not be negative and should be given at a time which allows for correction and rebuilding of confidence before the next game. There is always something good that a coach can say or an area of improvement that she can point towards. Punishments or negative criticisms do not encourage the kind of involvement that we believe is necessary for a team to enjoy working together.

We feel that coaching is about helping players to believe in their own ability and to know their weaknesses, but also to feel that support is available to help them develop and improve.

Anxiety about performance is a common problem with all competitors and soon expresses itself in a less than optimum performance. Players need to be helped to be able to relax, to think about themselves in a confident way and to recognise in their own behaviour signs of tension and worry. Coaches too should watch for obvious signs of anxiety, such as muscle tension or increased respiration, and identify what might help a player to relax just enough to allow good play. There are many techniques, such as progressive relaxation and mental rehearsal, which can help players train themselves, not only to recognise when they are not mentally ready for play, but also, and more important, help them to develop strategies to cope with, and control how they feel.

The trick is to channel negative tensions and anxiety and change them into positive feelings which will motivate and energise performance. This kind of skill takes just as long to develop as the physical skills we spend so much time practising.

Preparation for competition therefore involves the individual in setting themselves into the right mood before the game begins. All kinds of obstacles might need to be removed before a player can concentrate on her play. For example, they may have had problems in everyday life to cope with, or feel distracted by other demands on their time, such as their studies, their job or personal relationships. It may even be a problem as simple as arriving late or forgetting to bring a pair of socks!

Another aspect players now need to cope with is the ability to prepare themselves for games in which they might find themselves starting as a substitute or being substituted during the game. Their mental approach to this is crucial, since either situation can cause extra anxieties and tension. Keeping a positive approach to the game is harder when a player is physically removed from the field.

During a game there are also moments which are more difficult to cope with, such as just after a goal has been scored against you, or when a move has broken down or a shot saved. Each player has to be able to lift herself at these moments and stay mentally tough. Everyone has seen players who collapse at such times, either physically, in the way they hold their stick and drop their heads, or mentally, either losing concentration and fumbling the ball, avoiding involvement in play, or, even worse, blaming team-mates for poor performance.

Sometimes players can become uncoachable because they constantly deflect blame and responsibility from their own performance. These players need help to accept that they must look first at their own play and see what needs to be done to improve. Excuses are a smoke screen which prevents progress. Sometimes the 'valley of excuses' is a way of absolving oneself from responsibility and from involvement with the team. It can also be a way of explaining bad behaviour on the field since opponents are cited as the reason, or excuse, for an inexcusable retaliation.

Generally, a positive attitude is best developed when everyone, coach and players, maintains a balanced approach to the game and keeps it in context. Commitment and dedication are vital if players are to improve and develop, but a balanced view of life is just as important if over-intensity and narrowness are to be avoided. This leads to a consideration of players' and coaches' attitudes towards winning and losing. A coach should aim to strike a balance between players being 'frightened to lose' and 'wanting to win too much'. Both these mental states are negative factors in the pursuit of success.

Setting goals for individuals is important so that smaller, more realistic achievements can be attained. If players can focus on goals for themselves in terms of skills to be achieved – both mental and physical – then motivation and satisfaction should remain high.

Goal setting should be an enabling device which allows players to practise their best performances. It should not present them with too little or too much to achieve. 'One step at a time' is a good maxim for any coach.

Coaches must be aware of the differences between 'performance goals' and 'outcome goals'. Performance goals focus attention on improving individual and team performance in relation to past play, where-as outcome goals focus on results. It is easy to see that too much emphasis on outcome goals could demoralise players and put attention only on victory as reward. There are many other rewards that can be valued by coach and players, such as praise and noting improvement and effort. Players can be encouraged to feel satisfaction in the achievement of a new skill or tactic that is used successfully in the game. All these can be commented upon and seen as valued elements in the build-up to success. A team that receives positive feedback, has challenges given to them that they can relate to, and sees success as a progressive series of achievements, will be happier and more relaxed in their approach to training and competition.

'One of the things that an athlete needs to accept is the fact that success comes in many ways, one of which is winning.' D. V. Harris and B. L. Harris, *An Athlete's Guide to Sports Psychology: Mental Skills for Physical People*, Leisure Press 1984.

Concentration *(Fig 124)*

One of the problems facing individual players and teams is the multitude of distractions that can impair their performance. Players need to be helped to acquire the ability to concentrate on essentials and ignore obstacles that can deflect their focus. This is particularly important on the field where a lapse in concentration could be critical.

How can players stay on track when there seem to be so many potential distractions? And what kind of distractions should we look out for?

Fig 124   A study in player concentration.

Off the Field

Stress in other spheres of life.
Plateaux in performance or lack of motivation.
Niggling injuries.
Irritations caused by your own or other's lack of organisation.
Friction between individuals.
Anxiety.

On the Field

Temporary breakdown of skill performance.
Contested umpiring decisions.
Opponent's apparent roughness.
Use of verbal abuse.
Changes in the score line at a crucial point in the game.
Poor playing conditions.
Stoppage of play for injury, etc.
Substitution processes within the game.

There will always be distractions, but players need to be able to turn every negative into a positive and to accommodate or, if possible, remove the distraction itself. How can players develop the mental toughness required to do this?

Coaching

1. Players need to *recognise* the distraction for what it is. The coach can help here by talking to players about the things that can act as a distraction, or even by setting up situations which will give them practice at coping. Sometimes an incident can be used to advantage as a focus for discussion. This could be related to problems an individual player is having, or situations likely to be met when competing against a particular team. Players could be encouraged to jot down memories of their feelings, before and during a game, to see what caused a distraction and whether they felt able to cope. Coaches too are not exempt from the need to recognise distractions that affect their performance.

2. After recognising the distraction, players need to be able to *dismiss* the situation so that it no longer impinges upon their performance. The problem or distraction has to be dealt with in a positive way so that the player changes her attitude from 'being influenced' to 'influencing'. The problem must be forced to recede so that performance can continue. Coaches can help here because a confident and supported player will have the strength to say, 'No – this will not affect me'. A mental picture of a player keeping on track, whatever appears on either side, might help a team get the idea.

3. The act of dismissing the distraction is helped by *focusing* on something else. This must be something that ties them in to the next job to be done. For example, an attack missing the goal could be distracted by this and 'slump'. If she recognises this possibility and immediately focuses on marking back, she could well force a turnover and score.

This sequence of events can be used as a quick reminder for players once it has been discussed and rehearsed. Just the words

'*Recognise, dismiss, focus*' could alert the team to a possible lack of concentration, or could help a team-mate if another player sensed disappointment or frustration at any point in the game.

The use of imagery can also help players develop concentration. This could be a mental rehearsal involving thinking about all the possible aspects of the performance or game that lies ahead. Going through the situations that could arise allows a player to anticipate the events of the game. She can rehearse in an active way her desired responses and attempt to foresee all the opponent's tactical and technical styles. A player can visualise in her mind's eye good performances that have occurred and use this feeling of confidence and satisfaction to set up positive attitudes for the ensuing game. The subconscious mind does not seem to be able to distinguish between events that actually happen and those that are imagined or dreamed. So the more often we rehearse or visualise situations that we want to occur, the more the mind will recognise them as reality and expect them to happen again. These are skills that players can practise without any physical exertion yet the effects very often can be seen in future physical performance.

This aspect of practice could be extremely useful for players who are injured or physically exhausted but could still benefit tactically and technically from mental imagery. When players are unable to practise as a team, the imagined run-through of a tactic could help bridge the gap until that team next get together.

An imagined successful performance of a skill may help deflect the well-known situation where a mistake seems to become contagious. For example, the vision of a dropped catch can be immediately blocked out by all players and a successful catch visualised. Here is a technique for 'dismiss and focus'.

It is important to recognise that mental and physical skills must both be practised if performance is to improve.

Communication

Good communication channels are vital if a team is to work and develop effectively as a unit. They must be planned for by the coach since it is easy to ignore this aspect of team harmony.

A coach can initiate good communication by being at all times open to suggestions and feedback from the players. This could start in practices where, after setting work to be covered, the coach asks the players how things are working, whether they have found any other possibilities, and so on. Talking about techniques and tactics is a good place to establish that everyone's views are valid and important. Coaching techniques, such as using questions rather than commands, setting problems to be worked on rather than giving set answers, all encourage interaction.

There are other situations where communication can perhaps be a little more difficult. A coach has to show consistency in her approach to players, particularly where some sort of criticism may be implied. We strongly believe that constructive criticism is the only way to enhance communication. Negative comments can be discouraging to both a player's motivation and their willingness to talk openly. A comment such as, 'Your shooting is coming along well, now let's think how to get those close in shots a little quicker. We could work on . . .' is so much more encouraging than a comment which is all negative. Obviously, there is always room for improvement but, in general, progress can always be commented

upon before giving pointers on how a player might work to get better.

Messages with a negative overtone need not always be verbal. We communicate a great deal by our stance and facial expression. Players and coaches need to be aware of this since it can affect the ensuing verbal communication. A 'closed' body attitude, a frown, or a turn away from someone can immediately indicate rejection. Right away the possibility of open discussion has disappeared.

Sometimes what we say may be clear to us but not to others. There is a danger of our sometimes saying too much or too little. Either can be detrimental to better understanding. Saying things in a variety of ways can be helpful since we all understand things in different ways and at different rates. This could just mean using different words, or actually presenting ideas through a variety of approaches. Some players understand tactics better if they are set out on a blackboard. Others understand best by doing them. Others pick up verbal descriptions quickly. Whatever the method, ideas, constructive criticism, game plans, advice, should all be set out as simply as possible, particularly at times of stress.

Choosing the right words and saying them at the right time could be one of the most important skills a coach or player can have if communication is to be fostered. Avoiding confrontation is also a useful goal since a feeling of 'them and us' can be difficult to overcome. Some players are good at summarising the team's feelings whilst being aware that the coach has feelings too.

Since there can be a variety of personalities and influences within a group, it is important that an atmosphere of trust is established between coach and players. Players must know that what they say will not be held against them, whilst coaches must feel that their position will not be undermined. Mutual trust and respect grows slowly and, once established, allows for greater honesty and understanding to develop. Players cannot communicate well with the coach and then proceed to ignore other teammates. The same atmosphere of trust and confidence has to exist player to player. A positive team feeling encourages shared ideas and ideals, and reinforces communication within the group. Many have experienced the negative influence of so-called cliques where communication is reserved for a select few. Whether or not everyone gets on well with everyone else, it is important that enough lines of communication exist so that the group can function as a team.

Players need to identify one or two people to whom they can confide, and who would be able to recognise warning signs of anxiety. Mutual support is important, particularly at key moments when perhaps the team is losing, or is not playing up to its potential. An encouraging word on the field can make all the difference at these times.

The relationship of both coach and players with umpires is also an important issue. Both should try to communicate an acceptance of the umpire's decision, even if they might disagree with it. Aggressive displays of behaviour against the umpire only communicate antagonism and increase stress. What will probably happen is that the umpire almost subconsciously becomes more aware of that player or coach and future decisions could be affected. They may also become so stressed that judgement generally becomes impaired. It is unlikely that decisions will be altered, and players would help themselves and their team by giving non-verbal support thus helping umpires relax. Later, if necessary, they can follow the correct procedures laid down in the rules for queries and discussion.

Nobody is the perfect communicator. However, recognising the importance of good communication helps us remain aware of the processes, and not just the products, of sport and competition. Valuing and respecting other people's views and contributions keeps sport human.

Roles and Responsibilities

With this focus on valuing and respecting others it is also evident that everyone has different roles and responsibilities within a team group. However, whatever the perceived importance of that role nobody should be made to feel inferior. The newest player has something to offer just because they are new. The way they see both their role and the group as a whole is important, since others may have forgotten what it was like to be a new member of the unit. Players need to be helped to identify the positive contribution they can give and therefore to feel part of the work to be done.

Whatever the age or experience of players they should be encouraged to take responsibility for their general fitness, training and performance. Many players may find the rigours of training and preparation difficult to cope with and coaches may initially need to suggest how and when to work on their own. In the same way, there may be a need to check on fitness, injuries, and so on, but always encouraging players to seek help without being asked.

Sometimes players may not like either their role or the responsibility asked of them since it may not coincide with what they want. However, part of playing in a team is the ability to adapt and accept the team plans, as well as recognising one's role within it.

Some roles can be demanding and difficult. Being a reserve or substitute is never easy, but a coach can count her blessings when she sees a group off the field cheering and supporting those playing. Whatever the person is feeling inside, her role as supporter is vital. The reserve goalkeeper who helps to warm up the other goalkeeper as if they were both going to save every goal is making negatives into positives. That sort of generosity is important to a team atmosphere. Fortunately, now the game has substitution, it is possible to play all the group at least for some of the game. However, it should be recognised that off-the-field roles are difficult for most players and admirable when taken in a positive way.

The captain and vice-captain have important and complementary roles to play. They create a link between the players and the coach and can be crucial in giving leadership on the field. The way in which they represent the players and themselves can help or hinder the channels of communication already discussed. On the field they can often act as an attack or defence leader, reading the game and encouraging the team at difficult moments. Off the field their communication skills will be tested as they represent the players' view to the coach. A good captain leads by example and is capable not only of doing her own job as a player but in addition constantly works for others in whatever way she can.

Pre-game Preparation

A squad needs to meet prior to the start of a match in plenty of time to give the whole group adequate preparation both mentally and physically for competition. A coach should make a general check on health and injuries and must ensure, especially if there is a physiotherapist, that adequate time is allowed for individuals to be strapped or injuries treated. This initial gathering gives the coach the opportunity to assess the mood of the group and their readiness for competition.

Team Talk

The timing of the team talk may vary from one squad to another. Some prefer it earlier, in the changing room before the physical warm-up starts, and others prefer it later. There is no rule on this but the talk will be so much more effective if the timing is mutually agreed by both the coach and players. The talk should have a balance between discussion of the opposition and the squad's own game style. It is a mistake to overemphasise what the opponents will do, though in some cases it may be necessary to give specific tasks to certain players who will need to know before the day of competition in order to think things through. Coaches have to accept that for players not much is taken in at this moment and the talk needs to be short and to the point.

There is no way that a squad can cope with detailed analysis of team plays and possibilities. The coach needs to use more general attitude remarks and cues to reference some previous practice. They need punchy sentences to put across an idea or catch words that are repeatable and really illuminate a positive and motivating thought.

Physical Warm-Up

All players should work through a series of individual stretching exercises to prepare their muscles before explosive movement begins. The general stretching programme may vary in individuals as this needs to be related to past injuries. After individual stick-work warm-ups, unit practices for attacks, defences and goalkeepers will focus the physical skills, and finally whole-group practices can concentrate on positive reinforcement, group interaction and confident attitudes. A coach should use this physical preparation to eliminate negative feelings by choosing areas of practice that build up confidence and teamwork. Competition within the warm-up should not create feelings of failure. This can be overcome by working like with like, e.g. attacks act as defences versus their own attack, or goalkeepers are warmed up by each other or one of the coaches.

Immediately Prior to the Game

A few words prior to taking the field will give cues for action, focus of attention and encouragement in general. This is the moment for saying, 'Believe in yourselves! You can do it!' A quick practice together at this point will reinforce the positive team feeling.

Half Time

Whatever is said at this point needs to be simple and positive. There will be general pointers to all players, with certain things to focus on, as well as remarks specific to individuals. Certain players may need to do a special job or be in need of particular encouragement or a boost of confidence.

Substitutes

It is never easy waiting for the moment to run and become part of the group effort in the game. It helps substitutes to be given something on which to focus when they first take the field, as well as a short chat when they come off, if at all possible, giving them encouragement and keeping their morale high.

End of the Game

It is perhaps not possible immediately after the game, or even advisable, but at some point following a match an assessment should be made of what can be learnt from that total experience. It is vital in this discussion together that the team give *their* views fully as well as the coach.

Values

Many of the points made so far in this chapter are based on the twin concepts of respect and responsibility. We all have a responsibility to our sport and to each other. Playing to win is clearly one objective of the game, but if this is pursued too narrowly, much of the joy and satisfaction can go out of sport. A score line may be extremely important for one day but then is forgotten in the mists of time. The way in which individuals conduct themselves is unlikely to be so quickly forgotten.

'*Know the limits*' and '*know you have done it right*'. No one is saying that people should not do their best. Play hard, work hard to improve, to be more skilful, to coach better and umpire better. But this we believe is a process, and even losing is part of that process, an experience to be learned from in order to do better next time.

It is hard to respect people who perhaps, in your view, use unfair means to gain advantage, and there is no doubt that values differ in all sports between participants. However, if a team and its coaches know clearly what their values are, then it becomes more possible to resist the temptation to retaliate. Playing your own game establishes an important priority and standard and keeps your self-respect and respect for each other intact. The best matches are those where, by playing up to or beyond your own expectations, everything goes right.

Whatever level you are involved in it is important to realise that everyone needs to feel that what they are doing is worthwhile and appreciated. Remembering to acknowledge everyone's contribution is another part of the process of playing sport. Sport may not in itself make us better people – indeed many would claim that it can do the opposite if we look at professional sport today. However, what is sometimes not appreciated is that sport, because of its intensity and immediacy, allows us to show very clearly what kind of person we already are, and how we react in times of stress.

Coaches and players therefore need to work together to learn how to produce their best performances under the pressure of competition, so that they can demonstrate, in the most demanding and difficult circumstances, good conduct and a respect for their sport and all its participants.

Fitness and Training

There are several excellent sources of information available nowadays on fitness, training methods, and the avoidance of injury.

Coaches and players should recognise that fitness in its broadest sense is the basic requisite for good play in women's lacrosse. Poor fitness levels can seriously affect decision making at crucial points in a game. Injury can act as a distraction to a player's focus and concentration as well as having more obvious effects on physical mobility.

Most information on fitness identifies four major features:

1. Endurance, 2. Flexibility, 3. Speed, 4. Strength; (*see The Body in Action*, NCF Introductory Study Pack 2, p. 10).

However, every activity, whether it is a demanding sport, or just that required merely for living a healthy lifestyle, is composed of varying combinations of these four components. Therefore, every lacrosse player needs to consider what her sport, and her role, requires of her in developing total fitness. She also needs to consider what, as an individual, she has in her favour before she plans her training.

The relationship of the four components of fitness is important. For example, different sports require a different emphasis and relationship between each one. Speed is obviously needed in lacrosse, but particularly changes of speed over short or longer distances. The ability to vary speed may be more important in some situations than the ability to run faster than other players. Speed changes can be used to fake, or draw an opponent, before another move is made. It can involve running speed, quickness in changing direction, stick movement speed or combinations of all three. Players are naturally gifted or not in optimum sprinting capability, but this should not deter the practice of combinations of speed change within their own limits. Basic speed can also be improved through practice. Speed is not just a question of muscular power but of such 'game skills' as timing, anticipation and cue perception. These are psychomotor rather than pure physical skills.

Endurance is required so that high quality performance is not affected by fatigue. Lacrosse players are required to do many short bursts of activity during a game and each must be performed with skill and judgement. Basic endurance, or stamina, is built up over a period of time by developing aerobic fitness, that is, the ability to provide the muscles with sufficient oxygen for prolonged activity. This is done by continuous steady running for example, over long distances, interval running, timed distance running, circuits and general activities, such as skipping, cycling, swimming, etc.

When activity is done at speed and under pressure, oxygen debt results, lactic acid builds up in the muscles and fatigue occurs. Training, using repeated short bursts of activity at speed followed by recovery periods, helps to stimulate the type of situation felt in competition by games players. Training should combine both those activities which increase oxygen intake and those which help players cope with, and recover from, fast bursts of activity which cause muscular fatigue.

Whatever training is done, it would be wasteful of time, and also inappropriate, if it were done with no recognition of the nature of the sport itself. For example, a lacrosse player runs with a stick in her hands yet may be doing much of her training without a stick. Very often in a game the end result of a burst of activity, often at the point of muscular fatigue, has to be a shot at goal, an accurate pass or a safe catch. Training in shuttles could include relevant stickwork skills which would be practised for accuracy when the body is under stress.

Strength and flexibility are part of the fitness programme for a lacrosse player. Endurance and speed will be inadequate preparation if a player has not, for example, built up sufficient upper-body flexibility and strength to assist them in dodging and manoeuvring in relation to an opponent. Passing and shooting, tackling and intercepting, require general upper-body strength on both sides of the body and, in particular, arm and wrist strength. Fitness in general is helped if a player has good overall muscular tone, and upper-body strength should not be overlooked. Muscle fitness needs to be built up by increasing both the power and the endurance of the muscle groups.

There is general interest today in nutrition and a healthy lifestyle. Diet should not be ignored by the lacrosse player. Fats and carbohyydrates help the muscles produce energy. Protein helps build up muscle. It should also be remembered that even in a cool climate the body loses water during exercise and a player should maintain a steady intake of liquid to avoid dehydration.

Many an enthusiastic player can train hard but cause herself unnecessary injury by paying too little attention to warming up. This should be the responsibility of each player who should know if she has any particular weakness or stiff areas needing special care. Warming up can start in several ways depending on circumstances, but the main aim is to raise the body temperature. Warm clothing, gentle jogging, running on the spot, can all assist in this process.

Once the general body temperature is raised then important muscle groups can be stretched gently. Never 'bounce'. Take the muscle groups gently to full extension, and as they relax, go a little further and hold. Once the whole body is warmed up, then some faster running and stickwork exercise will help to tune up reactions and get full concentration on the task in hand. Players often develop their own ways of becoming tuned in and ready for play. This is an area that coach and players can discuss together since it is important that the warm-up feels right. It is not just the body that is being prepared, but the player's mental attitude to competition.

After practice or play a cool-down activity is also advisable until the heart gets back to normal. Gentle jogging, stretching, massage or a hot shower or bath, will help prevent stiffness and cramp developing in muscle groups which have been working hard.

Training must also relate to the requirements of the season. Players and coaches need to look at the times in the season where peak fitness is required. Pre-season training will often consist of building up general aerobic fitness along with basic flexibility and strength. Players may also be participating in other sports which have some common elements which transfer to lacrosse. Towards the beginning of the lacrosse season, intensive aerobic training should be built up with fitness becoming more specific to the game. There should be much greater emphasis on stickwork, specific strength training and flexibility work. During the season training should continue but be less intensive. One of the important elements in training is the maintenance of motivation. Some players find training difficult to do. Variety in the intensity and type of activity undertaken may help the more serious competitor who should be training daily. Even those who train less often may feel greater commitment if the focus changes regularly. Alternating indoor with outdoor work, individual with group activity, specific sport and other sport training can help keep interest alive.

Training, however, is a matter for individuals to develop in their own way, particularly when players have different lifestyles which allow only certain times and space for training.

Given the general guidelines available, each player needs to work out their own training schedule, though obviously it may be necessary at first to suggest programmes to young players and guide them towards suitable training for their level of play. Sometimes coaches could encourage good training habits by asking players to keep a diary, recording what they have done and how they feel about their fitness and stickwork, both areas that can be developed in their own time. A diary makes players think about how training can be fitted in to what can be a hectic lifestyle, and gives coaches a basis for positive discussion. As mentioned earlier, when looking at coaching principles, this process should not be seen as negative, but rather as a positive start to regular training habits. Start from what is there and build on it. Avoid criticising poor fitness levels or stickwork weaknesses.

Training is part of a player's long-term commitment to her personal development and contribution to the team effort. It should be appreciated by coach and players as one of the many hidden elements in taking part seriously in sport. It is the building block from which good team play can grow, and may make the vital difference between one team and another towards the end of a game.

8 Pop-Lacrosse

WHAT IS POP-LACROSSE?

Pop-lacrosse is an exciting, fast, free-flowing game which is the flexible alternative to traditional field lacrosse. It can be played in any area by players of every age and ability, including those with disabilities.

Pop-lacrosse is an ideal introduction to lacrosse, incorporating the basic skills and strategies of the field game, but using a more flexible rules structure which can be adapted to suit the group of players involved, the equipment and area of play they have available.

The Aim

The aim is to score more goals than the opposition by propelling the ball from stick to stick whilst on the move down the field of play and shooting into goal.

Equipment

Stick: Any lacrosse stick may be used.
Ball: A standard lacrosse ball or, for use with beginners' sticks, the specially designed soft ball.
Goals: Pop-lacrosse goal rings or any improvised goals, such as hoops, buckets, chairs, etc. Allow for room to play behind goal.

Playing Area

● Indoors/outdoors, on any surface.
● Use easily identifiable boundaries.
● Mark centre point and designate a goal area of approximately 5m radius around the goal.

Players

Suitable for mixed groups, all ages. Guide to numbers of players: five-a-side would be suitable for an area the size of a netball court.

Fig 125   Pop-lacrosse can be played anywhere. Here two young players avidly watch the ball at Covent Garden in London.

Basic Rules of Play

1.   Teams alternate taking centre pass at the start of the game and after each goal, with the opposition 3m away.

2.   On the whistle, the ball is 'dead' and players must 'stand' unless moved by the umpire.

3.   When the ball goes out of bounds, the nearest player brings it back into play. If indoors, use the walls to take the ball on the rebound.

4.   With a ground ball, the nearest player picks it up with their stick and continues play.

Fouls

1.   No stick contact.
2.   No body contact.
3.   No ball on body.
4.   No dangerous throwing, shooting or follow-through with the stick.
5.   No trapping of the ball.
6.   Ball carrier to release the ball within 4 seconds.
7.   Defending players must mark an opponent rather than the space in front of goal.

Penalty: Free position to the other team – opposition 3m away. No penalty to be taken inside the goal area.

Fig 126   *This form of lacrosse is played by girls and boys of all ages – indoors or outdoors – and on grass or hard surfaces.*

In case of simultaneous fouling or no player clearly nearer an out-of-bounds ball: take a 'throw' by placing two players on the boundary 1m apart and throwing the ball up and out to them.

Glossary

Back-door A movement from the opposite side of the field from the ball carrier, behind the defence's vision and towards the goal.

Ball-side The positioning of a player between her opponent and the ball carrier.

Blind side Out of the visual field of a player or group of players.

Bucket The formation of defenders in a man-to-man unit defending the area near the goal.

Circle The marked areas at the centre of the field (centre circle) and around the goals (goal-circle).

Connecting cut A move towards the ball carrier and away from the goal.

Crease The 2in (5cm) white marking round the goal-circle which players cannot cross either with their stick or body.

Critical scoring area The area in front of goal from which it is possible to take a valid shot.

Crosse-over A foul occurring when the stick or body of a field player crosses the edge of the goal-circle.

Cutting An incisive run to ask for the ball.

Draw The action performed by the two centres to start the game.

Double team The co-operation of two defenders to mark or dispossess an opponent.

Faking Any movement intended to deceive the opposition.

Fast break The tactic employed when the ball carrier has beaten her opponent.

Feed The pass to a player breaking or cutting towards goal to shoot.

Free side The unmarked side of a player.

Free space A sector as defined by two lines extending from the ball to the outside of the goal circle.

Goal cut The movement of a player towards the goal to receive the ball.

Goal-side The positioning of a player between her opponent and the opponent's goal.

Hole The area directly in front of goal giving the greatest possibilities for scoring.

Man-to-man The tactic used by a defence unit whereby each defender takes responsibility for a specific opponent.

Open The description given to the stick head when there is a clear line from the ball to the face of the stick.

Passing lane   The undefended channel of space between the ball carrier and the receiver's stick.

Personal space   The space around the body that can be reached by an extended stick.

Pick   The deliberate positioning of an attacker's body in the way of a defending player thus causing the defender to have difficulty in staying with her opponent.

Quick-stick   The immediate release of the ball having just received to pass or feed.

Roll dodge   Having moved to one side of the defender and found the way blocked the player pivots with her back to the defender to protect the stick and change the direction of the dodge.

Set play   A predetermined sequence of moves by a unit of players.

Shooting space   *See* 'free space'.

Slide   The movement of a defender away from her own opponent towards another opponent.

Steering   A movement intended to influence the pathway of the ball carrier.

Stutter-step   A quick change of stride length and rhythm to wrongfoot the defence.

Tackle   A short, sharp tapping action by a defender's stick on the attacker's stick head or handle to dislodge the ball.

Trailing   Positioning behind the ball carrier ready to receive the pass if required.

Zone   A defence formation where the focus is on covering a space rather than marking a specific opponent.

Useful Addresses

The All England Women's Lacrosse Association is responsible for the administration of women's lacrosse throughout England. The Association has a national governing executive, regional organisations (territories), county organisations, clubs and schools.

Should any reader require information about the full field game of lacrosse or the developmental game of pop-lacrosse – the ideal introduction to the sport – please write to the following address:

The Chief Executive
AEWLA
Francis House
Francis Street
London SW1P 1DE

Other addresses:

Scottish Lacrosse Association
Mrs Rosemary Mitchell, President
4 Morton Hall Park Lane
Edinburgh EH17 8SN

Welsh Lacrosse Association
Mrs Margaret Turner, President
10a Cwrt-Y-Vil Road
Penarth, South Glamorgan CF6 2HN

English Lacrosse Union (Men's Lacrosse)
Rycroft Mills
Smith Street
Ashton-under-Lyne
Greater Manchester OL7 0DB

The above associations have co-operated in the formation of the British Lacrosse Coaching Foundation (BLCF) which has developed a structure for coaching qualifications at progressive levels.

Information about courses for coaches and the current register of practising coaches can be obtained from:

The British Lacrosse Coaching Foundation
National Coaching Centre
Crewe & Alsager College of Higher Education
Hassall Road
Alsager
Stoke-on-Trent
Staffordshire ST7 2HL

The National Coaching Foundation

The NCF provides a comprehensive service to sports coaching at both national and local levels. As well as the resource literature provided with the coaching courses, the Foundation's sets of six Introductory Study Packs and three Coaching Handbooks are valuable aids to new and intermediate coaches. For more information, contact the NCF at:

The National Coaching Foundation
4 College Close
Beckett Park
Leeds
West Yorkshire LS6 3QH

EQUIPMENT SUPPLIERS

T. S. Hattersley Ltd
Lacrosse Works
Weymouth Road
Winton
Eccles
Lancashire M30 8NN
061 789 1374

Peak Sports
Unit 4
Ford Street
Off Chestergate
Stockport SK7 0BT
061 480 2502

Len Smith's Ltd
36–40 Heath Road
Twickenham
Middlesex TW1 4DB
01 892 2201

Sports Activity Co. Ltd
Maldon Road
Danbury
Nr Chelmsford
Essex CM3 4QJ
0245 412907

Davensport
201 Bramall Lane
Davenport
Stockport
Cheshire SK2 6JA
061 483 3005

STICK MANUFACTURERS

Brine (USA) – plastic, adult and pop-lacrosse sticks: available from Peak Sports.

T. S. Hattersley Ltd – wooden sticks.

Sports Activity Co. Ltd – wooden sticks.

STX (USA) – plastic, adult and pop-lacrosse sticks: available from T. S. Hattersley Ltd.

Index

Other Titles in The Skills of the Game Series

◇ **American Football**   Les Wilson
◇ **Badminton**   Peter Roper
◇ **Basketball**   Paul Stimpson
◇ **Canoeing**   Neil Shave
◇ **Cricket**   Keith Andrew
  Cross-Country Skiing   Paddy Field & Tim Walker
◇ **Crown Green Bowls**   Harry Barratt
◇ **Endurance Running**   Norman Brook
◇ **Fitness for Sport**   Rex Hazeldine
◇ **Golf**   John Stirling
◇ **Hockey**   John Cadman
◇ **Judo**   Tony Reay
  Jumping   Malcom Arnold
◇ **Karate**   Vic Charles
◇ **Orienteering**   Carol McNeill
  Rhythmic Gymnastics   Jenny Bott
  Rugby League   Maurice Bamford
◇ **Rugby Union**   Barrie Corless
◇ **Skiing**   John Sheddon
  Soccer   Tony Book
◇ **Sprinting and Hurdling**   Peter Warden
◇ **Squash**   Ian McKenzie
◇ **Swimming**   John Verrier
◇ **Table Tennis**   Gordon Steggall
◇ **Tennis**   Charles Applewhaite & Bill Moss
  Throwing   Max Jones
  Triathlon   Steve Trew
◇ **Volleyball**   Keith Nicholls
  Water Skiing   John West
◇ **Windsurfing**   Ben Oakley

◇   Also available in paperback

Further details of titles available or in preparation can be obtained from the publishers.